ADIRONDACK CAMPFIRE STORIES

TALES AND FOLKLORE FROM INSIDE THE BLUE LINE

JAMES APPLETON

BOOKS

NORTH COUNTRY BOOKS

North Country Books
An imprint of Globe Pequot, the trade division of
The Rowman & Littlefield Publishing Group, Inc.
4501 Forbes Blvd., Ste. 200
Lanham, MD 20706
www.rowman.com

Distributed by NATIONAL BOOK NETWORK

British Library Cataloguing in Publication Information Available

Library of Congress Cataloging-in-Publication Data Available

ISBN 978-1-4930-7694-9 (paper : alk. paper) | ISBN 978-1-4930-7715-1 (ebook)

∞™ The paper used in this publication meets the minimum requirements of American
National Standard for Information Sciences—Permanence of Paper for Printed Library
Materials, ANSI/NISO Z39.48-1992

To the listeners of *The 46 of 46 Podcast*:

Thank you for listening to my stories and outdoor adventures from the Adirondack Mountains. I am eternally grateful to have the privilege of being a small part of your life. Thanks for loving, respecting, and appreciating the Adirondack Park as much as I do. This book is dedicated to you. See you on the trails!

CONTENTS

CONTENTS

INTRODUCTION

The Adirondacks, a six-million-acre park in Upstate New York, is shrouded in both beauty and mystery. This expansive wilderness is sparsely populated, with miles upon miles of untapped forests, lakes, rivers, and mountains. When standing atop these rugged mountains, overlooking its vast wild land, it's hard not to wonder what else is out there. What's hiding in the deepest pockets of the untraversed forest? What's at the bottom of the deepest, darkest lakes? What's lurking between the trees? Or better yet, what's hiding in the trees above us? What's outside our tents or hiding behind our lean-tos? What's crossing the trail in front of us, just beyond the glow of our headlamps? Whose eyes are watching us?

Adirondack legends go back as far as the first Native Americans and settlers who traveled, hunted, and settled this area. The definition of the Algonquin word *Couchsachraga*, their word for the Adirondack region, is both ethereal and haunting: Dismal Wilderness. It's this same rugged land that draws more than 10 million tourists to visit every year. Activities like skiing, hiking, fishing, snowshoeing, camping, canoeing, and kayaking bring outdoor enthusiasts from around the world. The Adirondacks offer a little something for everyone: from those who wish to spend a relaxing day lakeside to those who come to climb the tallest peaks. However, this picturesque wilderness holds many secrets. This land can be unforgiving, cruel, and even deadly to those who come unprepared.

The woods can be a friendly place during the day, but in the darkness of night, they can become something downright terrifying.

Many of us can remember warm summer nights, sitting around the campfire, in either our backyards, campgrounds, or deep in the woods, on the edge of our seats, listening to tales recounted by our elders. Scary tales. Ghost stories. Tales of strange and unexplained happenings. The kind of tales that make the hair on the backs of our necks stand up. The stories that keep us lying awake in our tents at night. The legends that make our hearts pound on the way to the outhouse in the dark. The myths that elicit fear when the wind howls or a branch snaps, awaking us from sleep. Do we crave this fear? Do we seek out these stories to satisfy our craving for the unknown? Do we really want to know what's out there, or is it more fun to imagine it in the deep, dark corners of our minds?

It is undeniable that this land holds stories, those that have been written down and those that have been passed down from generation to generation beside a campfire in the dark of night. While some of these tales are pure folklore, and others, wildly outlandish, many are hidden in a mysterious truth and darkness. This book provides you with a little of everything—Adirondack lore and legends that are woven into the very history of this park and new stories that you can read aloud around the campfire with your family and friends. It is my hope that these tales bring just enough fun to your next outdoor adventure, and just enough fear to keep you guessing about what's really lurking in this "dismal wilderness."

SETTING THE MOOD FOR YOUR CAMPFIRE STORY

It's time to set the mood for a good campfire story. Maybe you're sitting at your campsite around a medium-sized campfire, or maybe you're in your living room with dimmed lights and a burning candle. Wherever you choose to enjoy these fun, spooky stories, just make sure you're with good company! Here are the five steps to set the mood for a great night of campfire stories:

1. **Light your fire.** When I'm at my campsite, I prefer building my fire using the log cabin technique, but the teepee-style works, too, right? If you're inside, just dim the lights and light a candle (be safe, of course!).
2. **Get your favorite fireside snacks.** Good snacks are essential for campfire fun. You can never go wrong with the good old-fashioned s'mores! Dare I say, they're a must-have around the campfire. If you're inside, you should probably microwave those s'mores.
3. **Have a seat.** Pull up a log or a comfy chair.
4. **Designate the storyteller.** Choose whomever has the best spooky campfire-storytelling voice. Don't be afraid to set the tone, and lay it on extra thick and dramatic. Especially for the intro and outro of each story.
5. **Enjoy the spooky fun.** Sit back (or on the edge of your seat), and enjoy these spooky stories set in your favorite places in the Adirondack Park.

Now that you've set the mood for a proper campfire story experience, it's time to find out exactly what lurks between the trees in the Adirondack Park. Some of these stories are fact; some of these stories are complete fiction. Or are they? That's the fun part. You never really know. So prepare yourself for a wild ride through the woods of the Adirondack Mountains.

CAMPFIRE STORIES

CHAPTER ONE

THE NYE WOLF

⟵ ≪ • ≫ ⟶

In the twilight hours, as the sun starts to dip behind the mountains and its golden light kisses the surrounding summits, darkness engulfs the valleys below. The sounds of the forest awaken as the moon rises, and a wailing can be heard for miles. A howl that, to some, may just sound like the wind in the trees. But is it something more? It's best to be at your campsite before sunset, surrounded by the safety of others, instead of being alone on the trail deep in the wilderness, where no one could hear you scream. As you walk down the dark trail, unaware of what's following you, just beyond the shadow of your headlamp, then you hear a rumble in the brush, only to turn around and see . . . nothing. You swear you heard footsteps walking behind you, but the only tracks in the mud are your own.

That is how you know he's there. Watching you. Stalking you. Waiting for the right moment to pounce. The hunt is on. You're the prey. In these situations it's best to keep walking. For while he may not be fast, he's persistent. Cunning. Patiently waiting for the right time to attack a fatigued and unsuspecting hiker. But don't be fooled; there's a lot of false trails on these mountains. Taking the wrong path could be the start of a never-ending maze designed to wear out a weary traveler such as yourself. For Peter, straying from the group was his first mistake; being unfamiliar with what stalked this rugged wilderness was the next. But sometimes one wrong step down one wrong path is all it takes to find yourself face to face . . . with the Nye Wolf.

It was the summer of 1999 in the Adirondack Mountains. Hikers were climbing mountains big and small. Paddlers were paddling the lakes and rivers. After all, summertime in the Adirondacks is bound to bring lots of travelers seeking both solitude and adventure in the great outdoors. From the most experienced hikers, climbers, and paddlers to people experiencing nature's embrace and that "fresh mountain air" for the first time. Whoever they were and whatever their reason for visiting the ADK, they all had something in common: to see some mountains.

The forty-six High Peaks are the Adirondacks' main attraction and have been for some time. Climbing all forty-six to become an official "Adirondack 46er" is a lifetime-sized goal that many outdoorsmen and -women seek to achieve. Many of the High Peaks have official trails to the summits, and many of them do not. These trailless peaks, however, are often the scene of search and rescues as hikers find themselves lost trying to climb to the summit, unable to make their way out of the woods.

The DEC and the 46ers organization decided to work together to create official trails to the summits of these trailless peaks, known as herd paths. Some of these mountains already had makeshift trails established throughout the years from hikers following them to the summit, but they were not maintained, did not have trail markers, and were as rugged as can be. Map and compass skills are a must. Over the years however, side trail after side trail developed as hikers veered off the path in search of their own way to the summit on these trailless peaks, often causing confusion and creating lost hikers in need of search-and-rescues. The DEC and 46ers collectively decided to start this endeavor with Tabletop Mountain because it was the shortest trail.

Once Tabletop was complete, next came the two mountains that yielded the most search and rescue calls in the High Peaks, Street and Nye. Two rugged and confusing peaks, thanks to the abundance of false trails going in every direction. Street and Nye became infamous for their maze of paths, many going in similar directions, many going the wrong direction, some even dead ending or looping back in an endless series of circles. Without a compass, map, and extensive backcountry experience, it was nearly impossible to successfully navigate to either summit. Four-way intersections with nothing signaling the proper route resulted in lost hiker after lost hiker. Some were rescued; others, however, were not so lucky. There was something different about these two peaks. They seemed to swallow hikers alive, never to be seen again. Sometimes, nothing but their boots and backpacks would be found on the trail, with no sign of the missing hiker.

It was the middle of July when Peter and his small trail crew set out to establish one definitive route to the summit of both peaks. The crew navigated to the summits via a map, a compass, and a prayer. They worked their way up the mountains, closing off many false paths. They laid lots of branches across the incorrect routes signaling its closure while simultaneously eliminating the abundance of blowdown across the correct trail.

There were stories and rumors about why there were so many false paths on Street and Nye, but the truth had yet to be revealed to Peter and his gang of burly trail crew, unaware of what stalked these woods. It was assumed the paths were created over time from one lost hiker following the previous lost hiker's tracks in a never-ending cycle, forming the maze that became the trails up Street and Nye. The woods consisted of a beautiful, lush, open hardwood forest down low, while the higher elevation was filled with thick, rugged evergreens.

The first day was winding down as Peter and the gang began packing up their tools to head back to their campsite along the flanks of Street and Nye. Peter, however, wanted to cover more ground and continue working since there was still another hour of daylight, and camp was only a half-mile away. So the crew started down the mountain to camp, while Peter carried on up the trail to the next three-way junction to close off the two false paths. Peter moved up the narrow trail lined with tight spruce trees scratching at his elbows. He hopped over a fallen tree laying across the trail and caught his pants on a branch, ripping the pocket. As he continued, his pants continued to get caught on the abundance of branches along the trail, ripping them more and more every few feet. Unaware, Peter's pocketknife fell from his ripped pocket as he climbed up and over a boulder, just before arriving at the three-way junction.

Upon arriving at the junction, the wind began wailing with a light whistle as the trees swayed from side to side around the forest as the leaves fell like rain. This junction consisted of three moderately used herd paths, all of which looked like real trails. Peter was certain the trail on the right was the correct path, but to be sure, along with a general curiosity, he decided to audition the path on the left because all three trails went in different directions. A few minutes later, as Peter climbed up this blowdown-ridden, narrow, muddy path, the trail circled back down the mountain toward the three-way junction. Clearly the wrong trail, Peter grabbed some large branches and closed the left trail by blocking off the entrance.

As he laid the final branch across the dirt floor, something sped across the path behind him into the woods. Startled, Peter quickly turned around only to see . . . nothing. Then he heard rustling in the bush off to his right. The wailing wind started to blow heavily as he scanned the forest, wondering what animal was with him in the woods. Expecting to see a rabbit or even a deer, he saw nothing but trees.

Sunset was still another forty minutes off, so he decided to check out where the middle trail went next. Minutes later, as Peter stopped for a drink, he heard what sounded like an animal walking directly behind him on the trail, but he turned around, and there was nothing there. The only tracks in the mud were his own. "That was strange," he said out loud to himself, but he shook it off and continued traveling northwest up the trail for a quarter-mile, before it came to a quick and abrupt dead end directly in front of a twelve-foot boulder covered in green moss. This confirmed the trail was indeed a false path and his instincts at the three-way junction were correct.

As Peter turned to head back down the trail, something peculiar caught his eye to the left of the boulder in the thick spruce forest. Four backpacks were lined up on the ground, two black and two red. A pair of boots sat directly in front of each backpack. Three of these backpacks looked like they had been there for many years, full-frame packs partially covered in moss and leaves, but one of the packs was modern. It was red with a black zipper and looked brand new. "What are these doing here?" Peter thought to himself as the wailing wind picked up, blowing the trees around the forest and leaving Peter with an unusually eerie feeling in the woods. These backpacks and boots were out of place. Knowing about the abundance of search-and-rescues on this mountain, along with the long list of hikers who'd disappeared in these woods, Peter couldn't help but question what happened up here.

The sun continued to set as the golden magic-hour light shined over the green canopy. The wind continued to howl before coming to an abrupt stop. Alone and ready to join his crew back at camp, Peter started to walk away from these bizarre packs when he heard a loud rustle in the trees to the left of the trail. Eager to get back to camp to tell the crew about these strange packs and boots, Peter ignored the sound and continued down the path at a moderate pace. Something, however, was lurking behind him. Peter couldn't shake the sound of footsteps following him, but every time he turned around, there was nothing there. He kept walking, only to hear the mysterious footsteps again. Quickly he arrived back at the three-way junction, less than a mile from his crew and their camp down the mountain.

The sun was setting, and the forest grew darker as the crescent moon lit up the clear, starry Adirondack sky. After arriving back at the trail junction, Peter quickly grabbed more brush from around the woods and closed off this dead-end false trail with one final six-foot-long tree limb covered in green leaves. Both false paths in the junction were finally closed off. The day's work was complete. It was time to head back to camp and meet his crew for dinner. Peter grabbed his headlamp from inside his pack and flipped it on, illuminating the woods around him.

Suddenly the woods felt different. As he started walking, he heard the familiar footsteps approaching him from behind, only this time they were accompanied by a low, guttural growl. Peter's eyes widened as he stopped dead in his tracks, knowing a large predator was directly behind him. Slowly and cautiously, he turned around, his headlamp illuminating the trail, unsure of what he was going to see. Peter found himself standing eye to eye with the Nye Wolf.

The beast viciously growled as its black fur camouflaged itself against the darkness of the surrounding forest. The light reflected off its sharp white teeth, and a glow from its single purple eye lit up the woods as he locked eyes with Peter. This was no ordinary wolf. Slowly and steadily, the creature inched closer and closer, growling and snarling. Peter found himself trapped. The handsaw he brought with him was on the ground to the left of the wolf, and all he could think to do was to grab his knife. So Peter slowly reached into his back pocket, only to learn the knife fell out of his ripped pocket somewhere along the trail. As Peter began to panic, the black-furred wolf stopped and started to back away into the darkness. The wolf's glowing single purple eye remained locked on Peter, but as it neared the shadow line of Peter's light, it vanished into thin air. Frightened and unsure of what he just witnessed, Peter breathed a short sigh of relief and disbelief. The woods grew deathly silent for a moment; Peter's heart, however, was beating a mile a minute. He took another deep breath to calm his nerves.

The wind continued to blow as Peter gathered himself, but after taking a few steps down the dark trail, he heard that low, guttural growl once again. This time it was louder and closer. Before Peter could turn around, the wolf leapt from the darkness and attacked! It sunk its sharp canine teeth into the back of Peter's left leg, just below his knee, mercilessly attacking. The wolf continued clamping down its sharp teeth into Peter's leg. Blood ran down his limb while Peter began to fight it off with nearby sticks and his bare hands. Peter grabbed the beast by the head and with a strange amount of ease was able to pull its jaws open to release his bloodied leg before he threw the attacking wolf off the trail and into the brush. Peter's calf bled as he hobbled to his feet and stumbled backward away from the wolf.

The woods were quiet again as Peter breathed heavily. He fumbled to recenter the headlamp on his head so he could see the wolf, whose black fur kept it hidden in the thick, dark woods. Peter searched the woods left and right, but the purple shine from the beast's eye was nowhere to be found. Peter grabbed his handsaw for protection. The wind picked up, and without warning, the wolf attacked again, waging its strike from the opposite side of the trail behind Peter.

Blindsided by the crafty beast, Peter continued to fight off the attack. This time, the wolf latched onto Peter's forearm, causing him to drop the handsaw as the wolf dug its jagged teeth deeper into his flesh and began to drag him off the trail into the brush. Defenseless once again, Peter couldn't do anything but fight off the wolf with his bare hands. Like the first attack, Peter was able to throw the wolf away with surprising ease.

The wolf's attack was cunning and calculated, but the beast was old and weak, allowing Peter to fend it off without weapons. After being tossed down the trail, the purple-eyed wolf slowly got to its feet and backed up toward the darkness, again staring straight into Peter's eyes before it disappeared into the night, as if it evaporated into thin air.

The forest was quiet and calm now. Unsure of the wolf's whereabouts, Peter scanned the tree line, lighting up the woods with his flashlight as he looked for the predator. He prepared for another attack, but the wolf was nowhere to be found. Perhaps Peter had fought it off once and for all. Quickly he picked up his handsaw off the ground, readjusted his backpack, and limped his way down the trail. He had to get back to the campsite.

As he hobbled down the dirt path, with blood dripping out of his arm and leg, all Peter thought about was how shockingly easy it was to fend off the attacking wolf. Peter's mind was racing, and he painfully limped with each step.

Nearing his camp, yet again he could hear footsteps following on the trail behind him. Stalking him. It sounded so close that he closed his eyes and braced for an attack from behind. He worked up the courage to fight the wolf nipping at his heels, but when he stopped and turned around, there was nothing there but darkness. The only footprints were his own. No wolf tracks anywhere to be found. Peter's mind continued to race, wondering if he was going crazy. The wounds on his arm and leg told him otherwise. He was injured and alone in the woods, though he didn't feel alone. Peter didn't let his guard down, however, and as he turned back toward the trail, there it was. The beast's purple glowing eye stared into Peter's, standing only feet in front of him. The wolf leapt at Peter and attacked for the third time, but this time Peter was ready and easily knocked the wolf away midair. Peter moved past the wolf, which laid just to the side of the trail. He was only one hundred yards from the campsite and could see the lights from his crew. Safety was in sight, but he still had to get there. He took a deep breath, blocked out the pain, and kept moving through the rugged terrain. Around the boulders, down the ledges, and over the trees. Peter moved as fast as he could, and he yelled to his crew for help.

Peter's crew was finishing up dinner when they heard his cry. Immediately they ran to his aid. His calf and forearm continued to bleed profusely, so the crew bandaged his wounds and remained on high alert, for the wolf could be anywhere. Despite their exhaustion, they packed up camp. They called the rangers for help and told them what happened. Ironically, while working on the trails up Street and Nye to limit the search-and-rescues, Peter became the next person needing a rescue.

The crew helped Peter down the trail to Indian Pass Brook, where they were met by multiple rangers and a helicopter to take Peter away. Whatever attacked Peter on Nye Mountain was still up there, and they weren't going back to find out where. Peter was fortunate that he didn't become the next hiker to go missing on the flanks of Street and Nye like so many in the past. He was able to fend off the beast and live to see another day. While Peter was being flown to safety, his forearm and leg in tourniquets, the ranger in the helicopter told him stories of hikers going missing frequently back in the '70s and '80s, never to be found again. He even told stories of rangers before him finding missing hikers' backpacks and boots but no signs of the hikers themselves. Almost as if they'd vanished into thin air.

The story was coming together now as Peter continued to fight off the pain after his run-in with the Nye Wolf. A wolf so cunning and persistent yet surprisingly easy to fight off. A stealthy and intuitive beast. Peter thought about where he was attacked, with the initial assault coming immediately after he closed off the two false herd paths, paths the Nye Wolf may have created for its own survival. After all, a lost and confused hiker is an easy target.

The story continued to reveal itself to Peter; the boots and backpacks at the dead-end trail, followed by the initial attack once he closed the trail. Peter learned what stalks the woods of Street and Nye. Where the false paths really came from. How all the missing hikers disappeared. It all started to make sense.

A hiker becomes easy prey when they're exhausted, wandering around in circles in a maze of trails. Lost. It's in these moments that the Nye Wolf waits patiently before moving in for the kill. But you'll never see him coming, of course. Peter certainly didn't. And neither did the dozens of missing hikers before him.

Half-spirit, half-animal, the Nye Wolf is a cunning creature who delicately stalks his prey. Masterminding his attack. The Nye Wolf has roamed the High Peaks Wilderness for a lifetime, but as time passed, his age increased while his strength and speed decreased. However, the wolf did what any alpha predator would do: adapt. The Nye Wolf's sly tactics to catch his hiker prey remain, but as the false paths on Street and Nye are closed by trail crews, it has no choice but to adapt again and expand its domain.

It's been said the Nye Wolf now wanders the entire High Peaks Wilderness. Some say they've heard its wails on Algonquin, while others have reported hearing its footsteps following them up Mount Marcy. Others believe it remains on the flanks of Street and Nye. Wherever it may wander, you can be sure its days are spent hunting for distressed hikers lost on the trail after the sun goes down. Deep in the wilderness with nothing but the glow of their cell phones to light up their paths as they desperately scramble to get back to the trailhead. The intelligent predator knows it's only a matter of time before the unprepared and unsuspecting hiker's phone dies. Going from a light glow one second to darkness the next. That is when it attacks.

It's hard to know if you're being stalked by the Nye Wolf. This clever creature is too smart to leave any tracks as it follows close behind you. Should you find yourself out on the trail, tired, late into the day as night draws near, just look back. If you don't see any tracks, that's proof that the Nye Wolf is close. As the Nye Wolf grows older, its speed slows to a pace even the slowest of hikers can outrun, and its strength is at an all-time low, so weak even the weakest of hikers can fend it off, but you should never underestimate the wolf's wit and intelligence A predator will always adapt to get their prey. His wails can be heard in the twilight hours throughout the High Peaks. A distinctive wail that some can discern, but to most sounds like the wind blowing through the trees. That is the howl of the Nye Wolf.

So, when you're out on the trail and you sense something following you, don't stop moving. Just make sure you get back to camp before you tire too much. Before the Nye Wolf wages his attack. Because if it does, you may never be found again; however, your backpack and boots will remain tucked away in the High Peaks Wilderness forever. A trophy for the Nye Wolf. A reminder that he's still out there. Stalking. Wandering the High Peaks Wilderness, waiting to strike again.

CHAPTER TWO

THE HAUNTING OF EAGLE CAVE

←——————— ≪ • ≫ ———————→

Eagle Cave. A dark and secretive place nestled deep in the Adirondack Mountains. For most people, climbing a mountain is enough fun, but for those wanting a more daring adventure, Eagle Cave takes thrill seekers inside Chimney Mountain to explore dark caverns and endless rooms lining the very depths of the mountain's core. A world of bat-infested blackness in which natural light has never touched. One misstep inside this cave, however, and you may never make it out. No one will rescue you here. For some, that's the thrill. For others, it's a recipe for tragedy. This cave system isn't just an untapped world inside of a mountain though; it has a history. A dark history. A history that incites people to take the risks as they climb into small crevices, traverse a maze of granite rooms, and venture deeper and deeper into the unknown, all for the reward hidden inside. Local legend has it the cave is filled with stolen gold thanks to a nineteenth-century Adirondack bank heist. Some even say it's cursed. For years, adventurers, spelunkers, and treasure seekers alike have gone missing on this mountain. Vanishing without a trace. Did they dare challenge Eagle Cave in search of its riches only to perish inside? Hard to tell. However, there's more than just darkness within this mountain. Secrets explorers learn the hard way once they choose to enter its depths. For thrill seekers Brent and Josh, they would discover more than they wanted to know about what happens deep inside Eagle Cave.

May 1, the unofficial beginning of spring in the Adirondack Park. After roughly six months of the cold, snowy winter, the season changes and unleashes the true beauty of this rugged wilderness. The leaves sprout on the hardwoods, creating a sea of green in the mountains, as the brown forest floor reveals itself from underneath the melted snow. The rivers break and run high, and the woods come alive like a symphony thanks to the birds in the air and chipmunks in the trees. It's a time of rebirth around the park, both in the woods and in the minds of those who wander them.

Adirondack locals Brent and Josh were avid adventurers. They explored this six-million-acre outdoors paradise all year long, but there was something special about the springtime. The shining sun in the bright blue sky, the varying shades of green trees, the grass, the blue lakes and rivers—it was a magical time of year that invokes adventure and excitement. Having lived in the park their whole lives, they were privy to local legends and folklore, but they decided to take their curiosity to the next level. Throughout the winter, they spent time researching one particular legend involving bank robberies, railroads, shootouts, caves, and treasure.

The year was 1891, and it's said a couple local bandits boarded and robbed an Adirondack railroad train carrying what was believed to be, at that time, $1 million in gold and cash. After a shootout with the train conductor, they escaped with the gold in bags and made it back to the Indian Lake area with their stolen treasure. Straight out of a Wild West film, the bandits were eventually caught and gunned down in a shootout on Chimney Mountain, just below the opening of a secret cave system known to locals as Eagle Cave, but the gold was never found. Legend has it the gold was stashed somewhere within the expansive cave system inside the mountain. Other legends say the cave is haunted and anybody who dares enter in search of the stolen gold will never make it out alive.

"I don't believe in that ghostly nonsense," Brent boldly declared to Josh as he explained the treasure's back story. "But what I do know is there's gold in that mountain and we're going to find it."

With gold in their eyes and adventure in their souls, the recent college graduates packed up Josh's red truck and headed south to the central

Adirondacks to Chimney Mountain. Having little information on the inside of the cave and being avid rock climbers, the two prepared for anything. They brought climbing ropes, harnesses, and extra headlamps just in case. After all, with no natural light inside the cave, they wouldn't want to get caught inside the cave without a light.

It was a bluebird Wednesday morning. The sun was shining, the green trees were sprouting, and the snow was finally melted around the park. The two enjoyed a scenic drive as they traveled from the High Peaks region south toward Indian Lake. They pulled onto a narrow dirt road that took them to the Chimney Mountain trailhead, where the journey truly began. "Do we really want to go inside this cave?" Josh nervously asked Brent. "What about all those missing-people stories?"

Shaking off Josh's nerves, Brent replied simply, "We'll be fine."

The two gathered their gear from the back of the truck and loaded their packs. Ropes, harnesses, headlamps, batteries, water, cell phones. "I forgot to let anyone know we were coming here today. Did you?" Brent asked as he waved his phone around the air trying to get cell service.

"No, I didn't," Josh responded.

"Well too late now. I don't have any service out here," Brent said as he shrugged it off and put his phone into his pocket.

They clipped their climbing helmets to their packs and began walking up the trail. The cave is hidden a hundred yards off trail, and without prior knowledge, no one would ever find the entrance. Thanks to their research and their digital treasure map in the form of a GPS, they knew how to locate the cave's entrance.

"We need to go 0.9 miles up the trail and look for a split boulder with a maple tree growing around it on the left side of the trail," Brent said as he scanned his notes on his phone. This was the first checkpoint the boys would need to locate before moving along the map to the next.

The sun was shining, the birds were singing, and the gentle breeze created a textbook spring atmosphere on the mountain. The boys found themselves in high spirits as their treasure quest was underway. With eyes glued to the GPS, they found the first checkpoint, the split boulder with the maple tree growing around the rock. Excited for their finding, they broke off the trail and continued following their map. Next, the boys had to skirt the side of the mountain for a hundred yards, where they'd look for a series of three boulders that signal the entrance of the cave.

They moved quickly off trail, crunching on last year's fallen leaves and blowdown, as they made their way along the eastern flank of Chimney Mountain. Soon something bright and yellow caught their eyes in the distance. They made their way toward the object, between the series of three boulders they were searching for. A yellow sign with caution tape around it read, "Do Not Enter. Cave closed per the DEC."

"Well, this is an interesting turn of events," Josh said, as they both stood at what they believed was the mouth of the cave. "Should we turn back?"

"No way," Brent replied. "We made it here and we actually found the cave. Besides, how do we know this isn't some homemade sign some-body made to keep people out of the cave while they find the treasure?"

Brent made a valid point, although it didn't ease Josh's nerves. The clouds started rolling in, and the breeze picked up, blowing the leaves around the forest. The boys walked up to the mouth of the cave and looked inside. It wasn't what they expected it to be.

"So . . . I guess this is the way inside?" Brent said, wondering whether this was indeed the entrance.

They expected to simply walk inside the cave, but the actual entrance was not so easy. It was a slice out of the mountain that required them to lay on their backs against the bottom slab and sidestep their way inside ten feet, with only a one-foot clearing in the crack from top to bottom. But this was the way in, so Brent took a deep breath, put on his helmet, and went first. He laid down on the bottom slab, holding his backpack in one hand out to his side, and started sidestepping his way through the crack in the mountain. The top slab sat mere inches from Brent's face, occasionally even grazing the tip of his nose. Taking deep breaths and trying not to think about tight space, he slowly shuffled his way through, step by step, as the light from the outside turned to darkness the farther he maneuvered into the crack.

Brent made his way out of the crack and finally stood up inside the first room. His headlamp shined around the atrium like a stadium spotlight, illuminating the cave's twenty-foot walls and ceilings lined with sleeping bats. It was cold and damp inside, the sound of moisture trickling off the rocks echoing around the rocky chamber. "I'm in a giant room inside of a mountain!" Brent yelled back with excitement. The feeling of adventure was real as he stood at the entrance to a secret world.

Meanwhile, Josh stood outside the cave panicking as he watched Brent crawl into the small, narrow crack in the mountain. Flustered, claustrophobic, and unsure of himself, Josh yelled into the crack, "I can't do this!"

"Yes, you can!" echoed back out of the crack, almost as if the mountain itself was speaking to him in Brent's voice. "And hurry up! You have to see this place!"

Too late to turn back now, Josh took one last deep breath, rallied the courage, and began crawling into the cave. He laid down on the bottom slab of the mountain's crack and slowly started sidestepping his way in. One step at a time.

"Slow deep breaths!" Brent yelled to him as Josh wedged himself farther and farther inside the crack. He closed his eyes as he moved to ease his mind and focus on his feet instead of the small space with only inches of clearance above his entire body.

"Just a few more steps!" Brent shouted as Josh approached the opening. He made it through the crack to the atrium and let out a sigh of relief. "See, that wasn't so bad, right?" Brent said sarcastically as he dusted off Josh's back.

The boys were finally inside the cave, and the quest for treasure continued. They climbed down some large boulders at the entrance as they moved through the atrium. The rocks glistened, the bats flew overhead, and the smell of moist, musty air filled the cave.

The first room was grander than they anticipated. The space was massive, complete with a dirt floor lined with jagged rock walls and ceilings. It felt as though they climbed into a lost world. Their headlamps shined from side to side as they searched the unknown of this new place.

The cave had an odd feeling about it, a bizarre presence that both Brent and Josh struggled to put into words, but neither wanted to bring it up to the other. Instead, they moved cautiously about the atrium floor toward the next room. Little was known about the cave's layout beyond some local stories and secondhand accounts they read online. They were exploring a new world beneath the Chimney Mountain trail. It was exciting and nerve-racking at the same time.

The entrance to the second room began at the south side of the atrium and involved crawling through a rock tunnel that was tighter than the initial entrance. This corridor, however, took some quirky body maneuvering to get inside. "I remember hearing about the entrance to the second room," Brent said. "We crawl through this tunnel, and it opens up around the last turn."

As the two crouched down and scanned the tunnel, lit only by the glow of their headlamps, Josh began second-guessing their plan. Unsure whether he wanted to trust the information Brent heard secondhand, Josh uttered, "If we get to the back of this tunnel and it doesn't open up, there's no way to crawl back out. You would have to crawl out backward, which would be impossible."

"Maybe," Brent responded, "but if it does open up, treasure awaits us, right?"

Josh's fear of small, confined spaces had him regretting coming along for this adventure, but after some convincing, he followed Brent's lead deeper into the cave. Brent got down on his stomach and started climbing into the tunnel toward the next room. He slithered like a worm through the small channel and around the rocks as Josh waited at the start. "It's tight in here alright!" Brent yelled back as Josh watched anxiously.

Suddenly the hair on the back of Josh's neck stood up as he felt a presence walk up behind him. Quickly he whipped his head around and stood up in defense, but there was nothing there. Only his own footsteps scattered on the dirt floor. He nervously scanned the walls and ceilings of the atrium, but as far as he could tell, he was alone.

"Weird," he muttered to himself, and he turned and crouched back down to check on Brent in the tunnel. However, Brent was no longer in the tunnel; something else was. Two bats stood halfway through the tunnel. One bat was facing Josh, and one was facing Brent. The two bats then turned in unison and reversed the direction of their stare as Josh watched from the tunnel entrance. "Brent!" he shouted. "Where are you?!"

The pair of bats then flew into the second room toward Brent. "I made it through!" Brent shouted, his voice echoing through the tunnel. "I'm in the next room!"

Brent's words were bittersweet. Josh let out a sigh of relief, knowing the tunnel indeed leads to the next room in the cave, yet now Josh had to gather his courage and crawl through. He laid down on all fours and started in. Again, taking slow, deep breaths, he wedged his body between boulders that have never seen the light of day, so tight in some places that he had to suck in his stomach to pass through. To his amazement, however, Josh made it out of the tunnel and saw Brent in the next room preparing his rock-climbing harness.

"It's about time!" Brent said. "Time to drop down to room number 3!"

The second room was circular, a quarter of the size of the first room, and a single medium-sized boulder stood next to a ten-foot hole above the third room. Brent began securing an anchor rope to the lone boulder so the two would rappel down into the next room. "Did you see those bats in the tunnel with you?" Josh asked.

"I didn't notice any bats in the tunnel," he responded as he finished securing the rope. "OK, time to drop into room number 3!"

As Brent prepared to drop down into the next room Josh noticed some markings on the side of the lone boulder. A two-word statement simply read, "NOW. HERE." The two stared at the message before Brent responded excitedly, "Great, we must be on the right path!"

Josh found the message to be a bit more ominous. He didn't feel great about the strange atmosphere inside the cave, but he was following Brent's lead as Brent began rappelling down into the third room.

Once Josh was alone in the second room, the mood changed again. The air felt different. A presence had joined him. His headlamp moved with his eyes as he peered from side to side. He felt movement next to him, but whenever he moved his headlamp, nothing was there. "This must be in my head," Josh thought to himself.

Moments later, as Josh attached his harness to the rope, he saw three bats standing on the lone boulder. He noticed something different, though. The words on the rock were reversed: "HERE. NOW." He wondered if his mind was playing tricks on him. Still feeling an odd presence in the cavern, he shook off the menacing message and rappelled into the next room. Brent stood at the bottom as Josh detached from the rope.

"What were you saying to me up there?" Brent asked.

"I wasn't saying anything. What do you mean?" he responded, puzzled.

"I swear I heard voices coming from up there with you."

They both looked at each other in confusion. Brent then informed Josh, "When I first entered the second room, I heard footsteps running down in the hole, but I didn't see anything when I shined my light down here."

This news put Josh more on edge, and he told Brent about the feeling of something walking up behind him in the atrium, the strange bats in the tunnel, and then the altered message on the lone boulder above.

"That's all in your head," Brent responded.

The two started moving through the third room. This was a long, narrow passageway about three feet wide and twenty feet long. They walked along the dirt floor, taking note of their surroundings, and the room came to an abrupt dead end. The boys searched for an exit to another room, lighting up the cave with their headlamps, but they didn't see a way out. "Well, I guess this is the end, and there's no treasure," Josh said in severe disappointment. "OK, let's get out of here."

Determined to keep the adventure alive and not give up so quickly, Brent scanned the room up and down, side to side, before locating a space in the rocks directly above them, an attic they could climb up to. "Look up there! That's where we need to go," Brent boldly proclaimed.

Suddenly the boys heard some rocks fall behind them from the hole to the second room. They went silent as they stared at one another. "What was that?" Josh whispered.

They reluctantly shined their headlamps into the hole, expecting to see someone or something moving above them, but there was nothing there except their climbing rope and a black hole. As the two stared into the darkness, two bats came flying out of the hole, causing them both to nearly jump out of their skin. Startled and with his heart beating rapidly,

Brent said, "OK, it was probably just bats. Let's climb up and check out that opening."

The boys wedged their left limbs against one wall and their right limbs against the opposing wall and started climbing toward the opening. Moments later, as Brent's head rose above the attic floor, a reflection caught the beam of his headlamp. He climbed a bit more and then saw it: a half-opened bag of gold bars and coins spilled out onto the floor of the attic. "Oh my God, there it is!" he exclaimed. "We found it!"

The excitement overtook the two boys, and they quickly climbed into the attic and stood before the lost treasure, lit up by the glow of their headlamps. Awestruck by their finding, they stared at the gold. "I can't believe this actually exists and that we actually found it," Josh said, catching his breath from the climb and excitement.

"Take that, Eagle Cave! We beat you!" Brent shouted, the sound of his voice echoing through the chambers of the cave. Brent then gathered the spilled gold coins and bars into his backpack. "OK, let's get out of this cave!" he said with a confident smile.

This was the moment everything changed. Suddenly a loud shriek filled the cave, and the walls started to rumble. "Whoa, what is happening?" Josh asked in a panic, as rocks started to fall off the walls to the cave floor. A horde of bats suddenly flew into the attic and swarmed the boys. Both Brent and Josh swung their arms in defense as they tried to get out of the attic. With no chance of slowly climbing down thanks to the bats, they both jumped while the walls continued to rumble and the echoes of shrieking bats filled the cave. It was ten feet down, and Josh dropped first, followed by Brent, who heard a pop in his ankle. "Oh no, I think I just broke my ankle!" he shouted, as he began limping down the narrow hallway of the third room.

"We have to get out of this cave now!" Josh screamed as he draped Brent's arm over his shoulder.

The walls continued to rumble and shake. Rocks kept falling. Echoes of ghostly moans, shrieks, and crashes grew louder by the minute as the curse of this Adirondack cave displayed its true power. The boys hobbled down the narrow hallway of the third room toward their climbing rope. Brent now had to climb back up to the second room of the cave with a broken ankle. Josh went first so he could help pull Brent up.

Once Josh climbed into the second room with the lone boulder, he noticed something was different. The strange writing on the boulder no longer read, "Here. Now." Instead, it had a more direct message: "Leave It Here Now."

This message sent chills down Josh's spine as the ghostly groans and shrieks continued to fill the cave. The bats were roaming aimlessly as Josh started pulling. Once Brent was back in the room, Josh shouted, "We need to leave the gold in the cave. Look at that writing now!"

Only this time, to Josh's dismay, the writing on the boulder was gone. It vanished. Josh scanned the room, wondering if he was going mad, but there was nothing written anywhere. "The writing keeps changing, and it said, 'Leave it here now,' I swear!" Josh shouted over the sounds of the chaos in the cave.

"We're not leaving the treasure here!" Brent barked back, "We've come this far, and I broke my ankle over this!"

The boys argued for a moment, but Brent was unwilling to leave it behind, and the two still had to get out. Leaving the second room with the lone boulder, the two crawled through the tunnel back to the atrium of the cave. The thought of going back inside that crawlspace amongst the chaos had Josh hyperventilating. "I can't go back in there!" Josh shouted in panic.

"This is the only way out!" Brent yelled back as he got down on all fours and began army-crawling through the small tunnel. Despite the madness, Brent inched his way through the confined space quickly as Josh paced back and forth. The darkness was closing in on him. The bats continued to fly past his head, and the ghostly echoes grew louder by the minute.

Brent made it through the tunnel back to the atrium. "OK, I'm through!" he yelled into the tunnel.

Brent could feel a presence sitting next to him, but he couldn't see anything there. Terrified, his flight reflexes kicked in, and he started limping his way through the atrium toward the entrance of the cave. Meanwhile, in the second room, Josh's headlamp started cutting in and out, flickering from light to darkness. His worst fears were coming true. The spare headlamp and batteries, however, were in Brent's backpack on the other side of the tunnel. "My headlamp is dying!" Josh shouted through the tunnel. "I need you to shine yours in the tunnel!"

No response from Brent and nothing but darkness on the other side. He yelled again and again for Brent, but the only sounds he heard back were the ghostly groans and shrieks reverberating throughout the cave. With no other options, Josh got down on his stomach and began crawling back inside as the tunnel flickered in and out of darkness.

Brent made his way across the atrium back to the cave's entrance. Feeling the unknown presence following him in the atrium and assuming Josh was only seconds behind him, he wedged himself into the crack in the rock and started shuffling out of the cave. Moments later, the darkness turned to light, and Brent was outside in the hardwoods of Chimney Mountain.

"Brent! Can you hear me? Brent!" Josh screamed in desperation from inside the tunnel, as his headlamp continued to illuminate the tunnel momentarily and then cut out to pure darkness.

His breathing increased as he crawled like a worm through the passageway. Every deep breath he took filled his lungs, causing his back to scrape against the tunnel ceiling. Instinctively he kept trying to lift his head up, but there was no space to move. The inches of clearance in the tunnel felt like centimeters. Josh's claustrophobia was setting in, and panic took over.

Suddenly a loud crash followed by a long, high-pitched shriek startled Josh, and he slammed the back of his head into the tunnel ceiling, causing his headlamp to fall off. There was no room in the tunnel for Josh to reach back and grab the fallen light, let alone put it back on his head. He laid there on the dirt floor with his arms underneath his body, wedged inside a tunnel inside a mountain, alone in complete and total darkness.

Meanwhile, outside the cave, Brent paced back and forth looking at his watch and wondering where Josh was. "Josh! Are you there? Answer me, buddy!" he screamed into the crack of the entrance. The only thing that answered him back was the sound of the wind in the trees. Brent knew something was wrong, and he had to act. Still thinking about the presence in the atrium, his nerves ran high, but he knew he had to go back into the cave and get Josh.

Before he started back inside, Brent walked a few steps past the cave's entrance and found a rock laid up against a tree trunk. He stashed his backpack filled with the lost treasure underneath the small boulder against the tree and then covered the area with leaves. This way their treasure was hidden outside waiting for them. He then broke a branch off a nearby maple tree and tied it into a knot around its trunk to mark the tree so he would remember where the treasure is stored. It was time to find his friend, so he walked back to the entrance, took a deep breath, and wedged himself back inside the crack for the third time.

Deep inside the cave, Josh remained lying in the darkness. Desperately trying to continue through the tunnel despite being unable to see even his own hands in front of him, he inched forward slowly, his hands feeling around the rocks before every movement. There was nothing he could do but recall what he saw during the flashes of light when his headlamp was dying. He tried yelling again for Brent but to no avail. What was supposed to be a fun adventure might be turning into how he meets his maker. He shuffled his body forward inch by inch as his head and back scraped the rocks above him.

"Josh! Where are you!" Brent yelled from inside the atrium as his headlamp scanned the room. No answer. Brent hobbled toward the back of the room and the tunnel. "Josh!" he yelled again, but he heard only the screeches and groans of Eagle Cave.

The glow of his headlamp led him farther and farther back to the end of the atrium, toward the tunnel. At the tunnel, he yelled inside, expecting to hear Josh's voice, but there was no answer. Assuming he was still on the other side, Brent started crawling through. After a series of unfamiliar turns, he made it out the other side, but there was no sign of Josh.

"Where are you, Josh?" he anxiously shouted. Brent then looked around the room with his headlamp, expecting to be inside the second room with the lone boulder where they set up their climbing rope earlier, but something was different. He was in another room as big as the atrium. "This is weird," he thought. He didn't remember back-to-back large rooms. He shook it off and continued yelling for his friend before entering another room.

This room was large, with two boulders and two climbing ropes attached to them draped on the ground. He examined both climbing ropes and realized they were theirs. Brent wiped his eyes, sure they were playing tricks on him. "How did these both get here? Two boulders? Am I going crazy?" he thought. "Josh! C'mon, talk to me, buddy. Where are you?" Brent yelled desperately now.

It was time to get out of this cave once and for all, but he didn't know where his friend was or where he was anymore. He kept moving straight through the unfamiliar room before somehow arriving right back at the tunnel he crawled in through. This time, however, there was another harrowing message written on the wall directly above the tunnel's entrance. He stood there, frozen in fear.

Back inside the tunnel, Josh's breathing was faster and shorter now. "Brent! Where are you? Help me!" he yelled, to no avail, as his blind-navigation efforts were failing and desperation turned into realization and acceptance of fate. Unable to catch his breath, Josh passed out inside the narrow tunnel.

Brent stood paralyzed, staring at the words written on the cave's wall directly over the tunnel:

BRING IT BACK

Suddenly the entire cave flashed with light, as if someone flipped a switch. Brent's head moved in confusion as he gazed back and forth around the chamber, searching for the light source, only to see an unending series of tunnels and boulders with climbing ropes tied around them. His eyes began blinking fast, but with every blink, the cave's shape shifted. The walls appeared to be moving.

A loud shriek then echoed throughout Eagle Cave, and darkness returned while the glow from Brent's headlamp remained. Seconds later, however, as the ghostly groans peaked, the light of Brent's headlamp quietly faded to black, and darkness returned, leaving the two treasure hunters lost and helpless. The cave decided their fate that day, and like treasure seekers before them, it determined that Brent and Josh were condemned to finish out their final days slowly, painfully, and alone inside the dark depths of Chimney Mountain's infamous Eagle Cave.

Brent and Josh were never seen again. They aren't the first people believed to be swallowed alive by the shape-shifting Eagle Cave. Adirondack treasure hunters have gone missing in these woods for decades. Were they all taken by the malevolent forces of Eagle Cave? It's hard to say. Some locals believe the bats that wander the cave are the souls of the victims of this cursed place trying to find their way out. The only thing for certain is that forces beyond our understanding dwell in Eagle Cave. The cave is alive and well, growing, changing, and controlling whomever steps foot inside. Be careful what you wish for when you seek adventure; sometimes something much more than the adventure comes and finds you. Sometimes the adventure you seek becomes your very demise. It was for Josh and Brent, as their bodies and souls remain hidden with the bats inside the dark pits of Eagle Cave.

CHAPTER THREE

BEWARE THE NIGHT AT THE COUCHSACHRAGA BOG

←———————— ≪ • ≫ ————————→

Couchsachraga. An ancient Algonquin word. Translation: dismal wilderness. A name aptly given by the Algonquin for the Adirondack region. Though maybe even more appropriately given to the mountain that bears this name. An isolated High Peak deep in the Santanoni Range. This infamous mountain receives a lot of animosity from those who climb it. Sometimes they're disappointed with the summit views, the swamps that surround it, or something else. Perhaps this mountain has more to it than meets the eye. Perhaps there's a vengeance it seeks against those who visit this dismal wilderness.

It may be the shortest High Peak in the Adirondack Park, but it's notorious for unexplainable things happening to those who walk its trails. Whether you're on a quest to become a 46er or looking for a trail less traveled, anyone who dares wander these woods will find themselves crossing the swamps that lay at its base, known simply as the Couchsachraga Bog. But beware; something changes in that dismal wilderness once the sun goes down. Something unexplainable. If you're brave enough to visit this peak, just make sure you're back across the bog before nightfall. Once the darkness arrives, so does something else. High up in the trees. Waiting for nightfall. Soaring through the sky after the sun goes down. This is a lesson that Andy and Sara would learn the hard way about this remote peak.

They'd soon find out exactly what goes bump in the night at the Couchsa-chraga Bog.

It was late September when Andy and Sara were packing up their green Subaru Forester for a weekend of hiking in the Adirondacks. This was the weekend they'd been waiting for. Not only was it going to be a beautiful, sunny, autumn weekend on the trail, but they were also about to become Adirondack 46ers. The culmination of a three-year journey. Sitting at 43 of 46, they had one more range to hike. A remote range that often gets pushed to the end of one's 46er journey due to its rugged reputation: the Santanonis. Panther, Couchsachraga, and Santanoni.

They were driving north to the Adirondacks from Boston, where they both worked as civil engineers. A drive they've made countless times over the past few years, so they had their routine down. Like most engineers, they were detail-oriented people, and they always went through their prehike checklist meticulously. Backpacks, check. Boots, check. Poles, check. Headlamps, check. Spare batteries—"No but I put fresh batteries in our headlamps this morning," Andy told Sara as he closed the back door of his Subaru. "Adventure awaits!"

They began their drive west on the Mass Pike to Albany and directly north on I-87 up to the ADK. It was a Friday morning, and they took the day off work because this was going to be a weekend worth remembering. They planned to arrive at the Santanoni trailhead midafternoon, hike into the Bradley Pond lean-to, and set up camp for their celebratory weekend. This way they could enjoy Friday night in the woods, hike all day Saturday, and hike out Sunday morning. It was the perfect way to finish the journey they started years prior. But then again, this is the Adirondacks, and these mountains don't care about your plans.

As they drove north, they passed their favorite sign in the world: "Now Entering the Adirondack Park. A 6-million-acre state park."

"That sign never gets old," Sara said with a big smile. They were both ecstatic and hardly able to contain their excitement about becoming 46ers. They turned off exit 26 and arrived at the Santanoni Range trailhead on Upper Works Road just after 3:00 p.m. Only two other cars were parked at the trailhead, which was unusual because this time of year is typically busy with hikers.

"Well, seeing as we don't have our tent, we're either sleeping in the lean-to, or we're walking back to the car," Andy joked.

As Sara finished gathering her gear, she saw a crack of light leaking through the side pocket on her pack, "Darn! My headlamp was on in my pack the whole drive from Boston."

It was unlike them to forget spare batteries, but because these were brand new this morning, Andy casually replied, "OK, well, we're not planning to hike in the dark anyways. We'll be fine!"

They swung their packs over their shoulders and locked the car. Their final High Peaks adventure was underway.

They signed in for the weekend and began the initial 1.8-mile trek down the dirt road before turning right into the woods onto the Bradley Pond Trail. The lean-to was another 2.5 miles away, so they hiked deep into the remote Santanoni Mountains. The sun was shining, the leaves were colorful, and the woods were filled with singing birds. It was a picture-perfect start to their weekend in the backcountry.

Sara led as the couple crunched their way down the mostly leaf-covered trail. As they approached the Santanoni Express Trail split, marked by a small cairn along the river, a solo hiker came rushing down the trail like someone was chasing him. Sara said hello, but the hiker seemed oddly shaken up and didn't say a word as he quickly ran past them. "Nice guy," Sara sarcastically said to Andy.

"Yeah, I can't believe he's out here without any gear, too. Not even a backpack. What a brave soul," Andy replied as the couple turned right at the trail junction heading away from the Santanoni Brook toward Bradley Pond a half-mile away.

The sun was setting, and the golden magic-hour light shone vibrantly through the orange and yellow leaves on the trees, illuminating the hardwood forest like a postcard. "This is perfect," Sara said with a smile.

The days were shorter this time of year than they were a month ago, a detail Andy and Sara both innocently forgot to consider when they planned their trip. It was unusual for either of them to overlook these details; nevertheless, the two picked up their pace to arrive at the lean-to before dark to conserve whatever battery life they had left in Sara's head-lamp. Soon they came out to Bradley Pond on their left and the Panther Brook Trail junction. They continued straight and moments later arrived at the lean-to, where there was a single sleeping bag and pillow set up in the far corner.

"No problem, plenty of space to share," Andy said as they both began setting up camp for the weekend.

The couple laid out their gear on the old, slightly broken wooden floor when suddenly two crows flew into the lean-to and landed directly on Andy's sleeping bag. Shocked and confused, Andy didn't move as the birds' locked eyes with him, silently staring as if they were looking into his very soul. Quickly he snapped out of his trance and shooed them away with his nearby trekking pole. "Damn crows," he muttered to Sara, who was just as taken aback by the encounter. They stepped out of the lean-to and began collecting small logs, twigs, and old man's beard to build a small campfire.

The familiar scent of a campfire filled the lean-to as they prepped their packs for the next day's adventure. The smoke rose into the clear, starry Adirondack sky, and it was shaping up to be a great weekend in the woods. The sounds of the forest were lively that night, especially the crickets. The evening was winding down, but there was still no sign of the lone camper set up in the lean-to. Despite not wanting to go to bed before this mystery hiker returned, they decided it was time to get some sleep because it was nearing midnight, and a big day on the trail awaited them.

They both zipped up their sleeping bags, laid down, and listened to the gentle sounds of the woods around them. Suddenly they heard a huge splash down at the pond. "Must be a beaver," Andy whispered.

Curious, Sara sat up to look out the lean-to and nearly jumped up out of her skin. The two crows were standing a couple feet from her staring at them once again. Neither Andy nor Sara heard them fly in. Instinctively, Andy grabbed his poles and clapped them together to scare the birds off. The crows flew away into the darkness, and the campers laid back down in their sleeping bags, sprawled out across the hard, bare lean-to floor.

A chill filled the air as the wind started to gust with no remorse, blowing leaves everywhere inside the lean-to and out. There was no rain expected, no severe weather in the forecast, and it was a clear night, yet the mountain was unexpectedly alive as the trees relentlessly blew side to side around the forest. Andy and Sara scanned the woods in wonder from the safety of the lean-to when the sounds of dozens of crows cawing mercilessly in the distance filled the woods. It sounded like a warzone. Andy and Sara's nerves grew as they listened to the ruckus deep in the wilderness, wondering what was going on in the dark forest. The heavy wind and cawing lasted only a minute before it came to a halt, ending as abruptly as it began. The cold chill in the night air was gone. Unsure what just happened, Andy and Sara nervously dozed off to sleep a little closer to one another that night.

The sun rose at 6:52 a.m., and so did the beautiful sounds of chirping birds. Still no sign of the unknown camper staying in the lean-to. Sara and Andy awoke around 8:30 a.m. as the morning sun shined in the lean-to. As the couple stood up from their sleeping bags, they were startled again by two crows standing at the front of the lean-to watching the campers. Fed up, Sara yelled at them, and they quickly flew off. "I've never seen so many crows in my life," she said as they began making their breakfast.

Nevertheless, the sun was shining, and it was the day they would become Adirondack 46ers. They took their time getting ready because they weren't in a rush. This slow moving resulted in a much later start than anticipated. More than three hours later, however, they eventually suited up for the adventure. Day packs on, poles in hand, it was time to hit the trail.

They hiked toward the Panther Brook junction to start the climb. They planned to hike the Panther Brook Trail to summit Panther first, where they'd eat lunch because they heard it was the best summit of the day. Next, they would hike over to the Times Square junction to out-and-back Couchsachraga, and finish on Santanoni, where they'd become Adirondack 46ers. A textbook plan for the day. But again, these mountains don't care about you or your plans. Especially the Santanonis.

They hiked up the Panther Brook Trail and refilled their water bottles in the brook before moving forward because this was the last place to pump water for the day—well, unless you want to drink the swampy water at the bog, of course. It wasn't long before Andy and Sara arrived at the Panther junction marked by a rock with the letter *P*, where they turned right for the final quarter-mile to the summit of Panther Mountain.

As they left the tree line and approached the summit, they heard something above them. Once they stepped onto the summit ledge, they saw two crows flying overhead, circling the summit repeatedly, and cawing viciously. Both found it odd because they've never seen so many crows on any of their hikes, let alone crows exhibiting such bizarre behavior. They felt as though they were being stalked by these birds everywhere they went. They shook off the weird feeling, however, thanks to their excitement for the summit and lunchtime!

High Peak 44 of 46. The end was in sight both literally and figuratively. Sitting on Panther, they had clear front-row views of the remaining mountains of the day. Couchsachraga sat below to the west. A secluded peak almost as if it was abandoned by everything around it. Then to the south on their left, they could see Santanoni. "There it is, number 46!" Andy declared to Sara. "Hello Santanoni!" he yelled from the summit, his echo bouncing off the wilderness below.

Immediately, a cold breeze swept in, followed by a huge gust of wind so powerful it knocked both of their backpacks over and blew Andy's hat off his head over the cliff.

Seconds later, the wind calmed down as abruptly as it began, and the temperature immediately rose. Annoyed, Andy walked toward the ledge to look for his hat, where he saw two more crows standing on the rock below directly in front of his hat. He locked eyes with them once again before one of the birds grabbed his hat in its beak and flew away. "Hey! Hey! What is with these crows?" Andy yelled as they watched the crows fly out of sight and back to the tree line.

With plenty of daylight left yet plenty of hiking still to do, it was time to get moving. They left the summit and quickly hiked down to the giant boulder back at Times Square, a well-known col and trail junction for all three peaks of the Santanoni Range. This junction marks the start of the unmaintained trail to Couchsachraga. Upon arriving, they snapped a few photos at Times Square and began the mile-and-a-half trek to Couch. They weren't anticipating the difficulty of the 800 feet of elevation loss over the mile to the col, so they traveled slower than expected. Soon they arrived at a place they read about, a notorious stretch of trail known to torment hikers. They were at the Couchsachraga Bog. A large, swampy mess filled with logs crisscrossing in every direction, deep murky water, and mud. A desolate area that looked like a tornado ran through it.

Andy and Sara scanned the terrain as they visualized their path to the other side. There was no obvious way to cross. This area felt different, however. There was something off about it, and there was no way to confirm the right way across this swampy bog. All they could do was start crossing. Hopping from log to log, small island to small island, they hoped the correct path would reveal itself during the trip across. Andy, however, couldn't quite shake the strange uneasiness he felt ever since arriving at the bog. The hair on the back of his neck stood up, and he felt as if they were being watched. Tracked. Something knew they were there.

He constantly gazed at the tree line, unsure what he was looking for exactly, but stopping every few steps to scan the woods. He led the way slowly and methodically, as the two made their way from one side of the bog to the other. As they approached the middle of the bog, there were two more crows flying low directly next to them. Paralleling their every step. Landing on logs nearby as they watched the two hikers cross. It felt as though the birds were taunting them as they flew across the swamp.

Another breeze blew in, and the air temperature dropped again. Sara felt the chill first and turned around to look at Andy, who was already checking the small thermometer keychain attached to the front of his pack. The temperature dropped more than twenty degrees as the two nervously looked around the quiet bog.

Little by little, they continued across, jumping from log to log and staying on rocks to keep their boots as dry as possible. Andy finished crossing to what they believed was the trail on the other side. Success. He turned around to take a photo of Sara while she was crossing. She smiled for the shot, but as he looked at the phone's screen, he noticed something unusual in the frame. Something big with giant wings sat in the trees behind Sara as she posed for the camera. Immediately Andy looked up from the phone toward the tree line, but it was gone. Vanished.

"Hey, did you get it? Andy! Earth to Andy! Did you take the photo?" Sara yelled as Andy remained lost in confusion.

His eyes frantically browsed the tree line along the bog, positive he saw something big, something strange, sitting in the trees watching them. "Uh, yeah . . . I think so," he nervously replied. Unsure whether he should tell Sara, he anxiously continued, "That was weird. I swear I just saw something huge with giant wings sitting in the trees behind you, but when I looked up, it disappeared."

Sara laughed as she finished crossing and told him to stop messing with her. "I don't believe in that nonsense; it was probably just a weird tree," she replied.

Andy was shaken, however, and given the fact that he felt uneasy ever since arriving at the bog, with the crows and the sudden temperature shifts, he wasn't so sure. Something strange was going on down here.

At this point, they were across the bog and the hard part was over—for now. They must cross back over the bog, of course. From here it was just a hop, skip, and a jump to the summit of Couchsachraga, and Sara's mind quickly shifted back to their quest for 46. Sara led the way, while Andy followed, constantly looking around the woods, unable to shake the uneasiness, causing him to jump at every noise in the woods. Every crack. Every chirp. Every . . . chipmunk.

They walked along the dirt path, but fifty yards from the bog landing, they came to a swarm of a dozen crows huddled together in the middle of the trail surrounding what the hikers assumed was a dead animal. It seemed like a strange place to congregate, but then again, everything seemed strange down here. The two cautiously approached the birds on the trail. Andy led, and as they moved closer, the birds scattered and revealed what they were surrounding: a backpack. Did this backpack belong to the mystery camper at the lean-to? Maybe the distraught hiker they passed yesterday without a pack? So many questions went through their minds because finding a backpack sitting in the middle of a trail felt suspicious and unsettling. They set the pack on the side of the trail and carried on with their hike. Afterall, they still had some peaks to climb.

Eventually they came out onto the tree-covered summit ledge marked by a brown and yellow wooden sign reading "Couchsachraga Peak." High Peak number 45 of 46. The joys of being one peak away from accomplishing their goal eased Andy's mind. They were close, and the final mountain was in sight. To keep with tradition, they stood next to each other to take a photo with the summit sign. Andy turned the phone around and quickly snapped the shot to chronicle number 45. Looking at the picture, they noticed a crow standing on top of the sign behind them. Quickly, they turned around and noticed not one but two crows now standing on top of the Couchsachraga sign. They never heard them fly in. The birds stood there, silently staring at the hikers. Seconds later, a third bird flew by, and the two crows followed suit and took flight. It was hard for Andy to ignore all the crows following the couple in the woods, and on top of the strange feelings he'd felt since arriving at the bog, he was tense.

The wind started to pick up, and the scattered white, puffy clouds that filled the mostly blue sky were now getting darker. There was much less blue than before as the sky quickly turned dark and ominous. Despite a weekend forecast of sunshine, the weather was shifting, although it's not like a forecast means anything in the Adirondack backcountry.

The trip to Couchsachraga took longer than anticipated, so due to their late start they didn't stay long. They were only one peak away from becoming 46ers. Sara clipped on her backpack and jumped off the summit rock ledge back down to the trail. Andy followed, but as he started to jump, another crow flew directly into his chest, flapping its wings in his face and brushing his nose and mouth. Andy came crashing down, landing on a root that rolled his ankle to one side. "Oh no, this is not good!" he yelled as he tried to take a step and immediately fell to the ground in pain. "This can't be happening, not out here!" he screamed in frustration.

Sara ran back up and asked what happened. He told her about the crow, and Sara yelled, "This place is cursed with crows!" Being inexperienced treating an injury in the backcountry, the couple didn't know what to do. They were deep in the remote High Peaks, so calling for a search-and-rescue would take many people many hours to reach them. As they weighed their options, they heard the sudden crash of thunder above. The sunny skies they started out with were now dark and storm-ridden, mirroring how their own hike was going. A storm was approaching. Andy had no choice but to try to hobble out of the woods. Being almost twice the size of Sara, it was going to be a long trip out.

So with no other options and in a race against a storm, they started down the trail. Very slowly. Andy hopped on one leg the best he could using his trekking poles like crutches. The sun was setting, and thunder continued to roar. They had to get back across the bog before the sun went down because crossing in the dark in Andy's condition would be treacherous. The two limped their way down, one step at a time.

Andy's anxiety increased with every step as he thought about the bog. That weird "thing" he swore he saw perched in the trees. Something strange was down at the bog, but he still couldn't articulate exactly what he saw or why he felt the way he did.

Each step required a lot of effort in this terrain. Too much effort. They needed to come up with a better plan. Time was running out, and the sun was setting. So the couple stopped along the trail to regroup and strategize. Andy didn't want to take his foot out of his boot due to swelling, but he realized he didn't have a choice anymore. He needed to wrap his ankle. Fortunately, both carried an ace bandage in their packs. They wrapped his ankle as best they could to give Andy a fighting chance crossing the bog. He loosened his boot as much as possible, and his swollen black-and-blue foot barely fit back inside. He was ready to carry on down the trail.

Moments later, as the couple took their first steps forward, a single crow flew in and landed on the trail in front of them. This time, the crow cawed at them relentlessly. The temperature dropped again, as an ice-cold breeze blew in and thunder crashed above. Their anxiety grew. Were all these birds a coincidence? Was this a warning? Were the birds telling them to leave?

Thunder continued to hit as they limped down the trail, moving slightly faster now with the bandage. They finally made it to the bog hours after leaving the summit only a half-mile away. The large, desolate swamp was lit up by the last light diffused by the stormy clouds. It was time to pull out their headlamps and pray the batteries don't die. The bog was dark, and the uneasy feeling of being watched was back. This time, however, it was thicker. Fiercer. To make matters worse, Andy was injured. A sitting duck for whatever lurked in these woods.

All they could do was move slowly and methodically. They put on their headlamps, and Sara led the way. However, only seconds after clicking hers on, the light slowly faded. Her batteries were dead. They were down to a single headlamp. This joyous day was turning into a full-fledged nightmare. Sara put her dead headlamp in her pack and wore Andy's. It was time to cross.

She began taking steps one by one, mapping out their route across the swamp. They moved meticulously like two engineers would, slow and steady. The bog was quiet. Silent even. Only the sound of the occasional swirling light wind gusts. Despite the eerie feeling surrounding the bog, their plan was working. Andy was in pain but doing what he needed to do to get across the bog. Sara would take a few steps first and then turn around to light up Andy's path.

Moments later, the mood changed. A chill was in the air again and the wind roared ferociously. They could feel the birds flying directly above them in the dark sky. This time, however, it was Sara who felt the uneasiness. "Something's not right," she shouted as Andy hobbled across the bog, using his trekking poles to balance on a half-submerged log.

Andy didn't want to worry Sara, so he never said anything to her, but the feeling was mutual. He knew they were being watched.

Andy moved off the log onto another dead tree, which immediately snapped, causing him to sink into the swamp halfway up his thigh as he let out a painful screech. He was able to grab onto a small branch next to him for balance, and he fought to stay upright. Half in the bog, half out, he tried to hoist himself up onto a log with his poles, but it was too late. It was at this moment when everything changed.

Thunder roared, and a murder of crows swarmed above, flying past Andy from all sides as he desperately tried to get out of the bog. Dozens of birds continued to scream and plucked at their backpacks as the hikers swung their trekking poles in defense. The crows were relentless.

"What is happening?!" Sara yelled out as she desperately swung her poles at the birds circling their heads. Her headlamp thrashed and flashed aimlessly around the swamp. The howling wind blew harder as the attack increased, and Andy and Sara continued moving across the bog.

Sara looked back at Andy, and then she finally saw it. Standing in the darkness at the tree line. Immediately, it launched into the air, heading toward them. "Andy! Keep going! Something's coming!" she yelled.

Andy immediately turned and caught a glimpse of the creature he saw earlier, soaring through the dark sky toward them. A creature so large he could see it through the darkness across the bog. It had the head of a crow, a man-sized body, and giant wings ten feet across. Its bright yellow eyes glowed in the darkness as its shriek pierced through the wilderness. The crows continued their attack as the creature soared toward Andy, getting closer and closer with every passing second as its giant wings flapped in the air.

Andy and Sara continued to jump from log to log, with little concern about where they were stepping now. Adrenaline ran so high that Andy forgot about the pain. All that mattered was getting across the bog. The giant-winged creature continued getting closer; its wingspan, bigger and bigger. Andy and Sara were almost across as the shrieking grew louder, the wind blew stronger, thunder and lightning crashed heavier. Sara finally made it to the other side and immediately turned to light up Andy's path, just as the creature grabbed him by his backpack, only steps from the bog's edge.

"Andy!" she screamed as he felt the pull from the creature's legs clasped to his backpack. Its giant black wings flapped above and engulfed Andy's body. Instinctively, he unclipped the pack from his body and slipped out of the straps, setting himself free as he jumped the final steps to dry land. Without hesitation Andy grabbed Sara's hand, and they immediately ran up the dirt trail, away from the wretched bog toward

Times Square. The murder of crows continued to scream, thunder crashed, and Andy moved at full speed as they climbed the trail. After jumping up the ledges and running the flats, they finished the one mile to Times Square in what felt like seconds.

The woods became silent. The crows were gone. With Santanoni, peak number 46, only a mile to the right, they had to orphan it along with their 46'er status. They turned left at Times Square, back down Panther Brook, toward their lean-to. They had to get out of the woods. The couple ran full speed for miles like obsessed marathon runners, only instead of running a race, they were running for their lives. They still didn't quite know what they were running from; it was unexplainable.

Down Panther Brook they went, back to the Bradley Pond lean-to, where they grabbed their other pack with the car keys. The mystery sleeping bag was still untouched in the back corner. Then out of the darkness, a lone crow flew into the lean-to, landing on the sleeping bag. It stared silently at Andy and Sara. With no hesitation they left everything else behind and ran down the Bradley Pond Trail, desperate to get back to their car. They ran the entire 4.5 miles back to the trailhead and never stopped once to look behind them.

Miraculously they made it to the parking lot, jumped in Andy's green Subaru, and spun out of the trailhead like bank robbers. The trip was over. Andy frantically drove down the backroads of the Adirondack Park when a large black bear ran out in front of them, narrowly missing the car as he swerved around it. Normally they'd be excited to see a black bear in the wilderness, but this wilderness was now a different place. A cursed place. A dismal wilderness.

Their minds raced as they tried to process what happened. What was that creature? Who did that lone backpack near the bog belong to? What happened to that distressed hiker? Where was the missing lean-to camper? What were those loud crows and sounds the night before? So many unanswered questions. The only answer they had was that something dark is going on in those woods.

Andy and Sara made it back to the Northway and turned south on I-87. A magical trip cut short. The ride was somber and quiet. They sat in total silence listening to nothing but the sounds of the road as shock set in. Eventually their heart rates slowed, and they were no longer hysterical. The couple shared a look, a simple nod, as they clenched one another's hand. Andy and Sara may never understand what they encountered that day at the Couchsachraga Bog. Flying toward them in the dark sky. Clasped onto Andy's backpack. But they learned that the forever wild Adirondack Park is wilder than they ever imagined. One thing they do know is that they will never return to that dismal wilderness, and they'll never look at crows the same way again.

Deep in the Santanoni Range, a place where missing hikers become yesteday's news, lives something wild. Something unnatural. Something unexplainable. In the forest. High up in the trees above the bog. Waiting. Watching. Be careful when you see those crows flying above. You never can tell what they're up to, and you never know if something bigger is lurking nearby.

For Andy and Sara, becoming 46ers might not be in the cards anymore. I guess they'll be lifelong 45ers. "Aspiring no more" may no longer be an aspiration. Hard to say if they'd ever return to finish what they started. Of course, if they did return, who knows if that same wilderness will finish what it started with Andy and Sara. What you can be sure of is that you should never cross the Couchsachraga Bog at night. But if you must, no matter what you do, do not step in the water because now we all know what goes bump in the night at the Couchsachraga bog.

CHAPTER FOUR

A SCARY NIGHT ON THE SACANDAGA RIVER

←———— ≪ • ≫ ————→

The woods. Often a place of rejuvenation to reconnect with nature to fill that primal need within us all. Whether you're hiking on a trail, swimming in a lake, or just stopping to take in the scenery, the outdoors can be a tranquil place on a bluebird afternoon. But when the sun goes down, that same wilderness can become a place of pure, inexplicable terror. The woods are a very different place at night than they are during the day. The forest comes alive once the moon rises in the sky. Things awaken and wander between the trees. That's why it's never wise to spend a night alone out there. You never know what's lurking behind your tent . . . only feet away from your head . . . with nothing separating you and the unknown but a thin piece of fabric. For Joe, what was supposed to be a relaxing weekend fishing and camping deep in the Adirondack backcountry quickly turned into a night of unforgettable horror.

It was a Thursday afternoon in late June when Joe prepped his kayak and fishing poles for a long weekend of fishing and camping in the remote Siamese Pond Wilderness in the southern Adirondacks. With the long holiday weekend ahead, he wanted to spend it out in the woods, the woods he'd explored ever since he was a little boy. The busy holiday, of course, meant bigger crowds, so his instincts took him deep into the forest where he wouldn't run into another soul. Plus, the fishing would be better. Joe was planning to fly-fish and catch some trout because they love to bite this time of year.

He tied his yellow kayak to the top of his trusty old green 1994 Jeep Wrangler with one red door. His car had seen better days, but it's also taken him all over the Adirondacks for many years.

Joe left his house and drove forty-five minutes southwest to his destination to launch for the weekend. He planned his backcountry expeditions meticulously and intended to paddle the north branch of the Sacandaga River, northeast of Speculator. Joe's destination was a remote stretch of wilderness that he was sure to have to himself. Or so he thought.

He arrived at the boat launch just after 1:00 p.m. He put his kayak in the water and tied up his weekend supplies, which included his fishing rod, backpack, tent, food, and cooler. Ready for a weekend immersed in nature in his happy place, Joe set off into the water but not before leaving his cell phone in his car. After all, what good is a cell phone when you're deep in the Adirondack Park without any service?

Thanks to his experience on this river, he knew the paddle would take him around three hours to get to his destination. It was a secluded area that rarely sees human life, just the way Joe liked it.

The river changed frequently as Joe paddled through flat, calm areas; followed by short rapids; and back to calm, peaceful waters. It was just him and nature. The trip included various carries over rocks and a couple beaver dams. Joe loved going to the remote areas that most people will never go because that's where the big fish live.

Around 4:30, he arrived at his destination and began looking for a good place to set up camp along the river. He paddled close to shore and found the perfect spot, a small twenty-foot clearing along the water. The air was fresh with a scent of the pine forest towering above and small thickets below. The woods were dense, and it was difficult to see more than a few feet between all the trees. A private nook with minimal visibility in any direction made Joe feel safe and secure. It was a place he knew he wouldn't be bothered.

Exhausted from the long paddle, Joe was happy to arrive at his weekend destination and set up camp. First he built his tent, a two-man blue dome tent he'd spent many nights in around the Adirondacks. Next, he began gathering firewood for the night. He collected broken branches and logs all around the campsite, scraping birch bark and old man's beard off the deadfall, and he piled it up in his campsite.

It was after 8 o'clock, and the sun was setting by the time Joe's modest campfire illuminated the campsite. "Time for dinner," Joe said aloud as he opened his cooler.

He was a simple outdoorsman and packed only the essentials: hot dogs and rolls. He found two sticks and roasted a couple hot dogs over the fire simultaneously, one in each hand. So far, the trip was going exactly to plan; after all, Joe had spent a lifetime in these woods, and he didn't expect anything out of the ordinary to occur.

It was 11:00 and time to turn in for the night. Joe prepped his sleeping bag inside his tent as the fire slowly burned out, and the sounds of the flowing river and crickets created the perfect soundtrack. The peaceful evening in the woods, however, was about to change.

Joe left his tent to put out the campfire, but just before he poured water on the flame, he heard three loud, crashing knocks in the woods:

BAM BAM BAM!

Followed by complete and total silence.

The knocks were loud, powerful, and fast. "What in the world was that?" Joe said quietly, having second thoughts about putting out the campfire. Confused, he listened intently to the dark forest, wondering if someone else was there. "Hey, is anybody out there?" Joe casually called out into the night. No response.

He shrugged it off and out of caution decided to let the fire burn a little longer while he continued getting ready for bed. A few minutes after the first, he heard a second set of crashing tree knocks:

BAM BAM BAM!

These knocks felt even closer than the first. Joe threw a log on the fire because this sound was too alarming to ignore. He sat silently, listening for movement in the woods. The only sounds he heard, however, was the gentle flow of the river. Minutes later, another powerful set of knocks echoed in the woods:

BAM BAM BAM!

Followed by silence.

"How could anyone else be out here?" he thought to himself. These sounds were different, even for a lifelong outdoorsman like Joe. His anxiety grew as he shined his flashlight around the woods, nervous he would see what was making the noise.

Thirty minutes passed after the last knocks, and Joe's nerves calmed. The fire was still burning, and he went inside his tent to fall asleep. Moments after entering his tent, however, he heard a large branch forcefully ripped off a tree in the woods to his left. Something was moving around, crunching leaves, and snapping branches on the ground. The footsteps were heavy. Joe could hear and feel a thud with every step as it moved toward his camp.

"It must be a bear," Joe thought to himself. He'd come across Adirondack black bears dozens of times throughout his life, but this felt different. The heavy footsteps and crunching in the woods moved closer and closer to the camp. Whatever it was, it was not being quiet.

So Joe left his tent again and threw the last of his logs onto the fire. He knew the bear would likely go away soon. The forest was too thick to see more than ten feet in any direction, so he couldn't get a glimpse of the bear. As he shined his flashlight into the darkness, he saw movement between the trees. A large, dark, shadowy figure moved from one tree to another toward the river.

"My brain must be playing tricks on me," he thought. His imagination was running wild, though he knew deep down it was not his imagination.

Time passed, and the fire began to burn out as Joe sat in his camp chair listening nervously for more movement in the woods, occasionally shining his flashlight into the trees around the campsite. He decided it must have been a bear and that it was gone now. He let the fire burn out on its own and went back into his tent to sleep. It was a long day getting this deep into the mountains and a long night now dealing with these odd sounds and what he assumed was a bear.

As he laid inside the tent, staring at the roof, he started to notice small pebbles hitting the fabric. Small stones the size of a nickel began hitting his tent every few seconds like clockwork. He even heard the stones landing on the forest floor, clanking against the rocks and dirt. This lasted for a minute and then stopped. He laid there like a statue, taking refuge in the false sense of security a tent offers campers. He told himself it must be pinecones falling off the trees above the tent. But Joe also knew there weren't any pine trees directly above his tent. He finally fell asleep and slept soundly until the morning.

Hours later the Adirondack loons cried, the sun rose, and the forest awakened. Joe began his usual camp morning routine, starting with the most important thing first: coffee. He unzipped his tent and stepped out into the beautiful summer sun and drank his coffee. The sun rose over the High Peaks to the east, and the weather was perfect. A comfortable seventy degrees and not a cloud in the sky. A bluebird Adirondack morning.

As Joe sipped his coffee, he thought about last night's events. The tree knocks; the branches; the large, shadowy figure. "That was strange," he thought to himself, before ultimately ignoring it and moving on with his morning. The sun was shining, the river was flowing, and he was ready to do some fishing, so that's exactly what he did.

He put on his waders, grabbed his fly rod, and walked into the river to begin the day. An hour passed, and he wasn't catching any fish near his campsite, so he moved down the river and tried another spot. Having little luck with the trout, he went back to his campsite for a lunch break.

Back at camp Joe enjoyed a modest meal, rolled-up cheese and roast beef from the deli. Fueled up for the afternoon, he gathered more firewood since he burned his entire supply the night before. The events of the previous night, however, began replaying in his mind. Out of precaution, he collected double the wood this time around.

After gathering more wood than he and even the next person camping at this spot would ever need, he sat in his chair and relaxed. He began pondering the night before, thinking about the tree knocks and how hard and powerful they were. "Maybe someone else is camping in this area?" Joe thought to himself. He stood up and started walking to the top of the ridge where he heard the noises coming from to look for signs of campers in the area. At the top of the ridge, his legs scratched and scraped up from the thick brush, it was clear nobody else was around or even could camp anywhere near him. His campsite was the only clearing among the dense forest.

He made his way back down to the campsite and came up with a plan to keep the bear away. The bear he was sure visited him last night. Knowing black bears don't enjoy strong scents or perfumes, he sprayed bug spray on the trees and the ground in a circle around the camp, as far as seventy-five yards from his tent. "That should do the trick," he confidently declared as he walked back to his camp.

It was 7:00, the sun was still high in the sky, and Joe decided to try his luck again in hopes of fresh trout for dinner. He suited back up in his chest-high brown waders and walked into the river. Like earlier in the day, luck was not on his side, and he didn't catch any trout.

The sun was setting as the clock approached 9:00, and he began his same nightly routine. The fire was burning, and it was time for dinner. Two sticks roasting two hot dogs at once. A true pro technique. While he was cooking, Joe kept an ear to the woods for any wildlife coming toward his camp. Perhaps it was the smell of the hot dogs that brought the bear in last night, though having done this a hundred times before, he didn't think anything of it.

It was after 11:00, and the sounds of the forest after dark were upon him. Coyotes in the distance, the occasional owl, crickets, the gentle flow of the river, and his crackling campfire burning steadily made up the soundtrack of the evening. Joe thought the night was winding down, but as it would turn out, the night was just getting started.

Moments before he planned to crawl into his tent, as he stood over his fire, he heard it again . . .

BAM BAM!
BAM BAM!

This time the tree knocks were louder, faster, and more powerful than last night. "Not again!" Joe nervously whispered. Like last night, the woods went dead silent after the tree knocks, before another set of tree knocks answered back, followed by nothing but the sound of his campfire.

Joe threw more wood on the fire and anxiously sat in confusion. Thirty minutes later, a large branch was ripped off a tree again, followed by another branch, and then another one. It was all happening again. Joe was scared .This activity was nothing he ever experienced. Definitely not from a bear. Desperate to scare off whatever was in the woods, Joe called out "Hello? Is someone there?" Silence filled the air.

He built up the fire to keep busy and give his brain moments of relief from the unknown prowling in the bush around his campsite for the second night. Fear was taking over as Joe continued to build the fire so he could see farther into the forest around his campsite. Despite the fire and flashlight, seeing very far into the thick woods was a losing battle.

Then movement picked up as heavy footsteps stomped around the woods. Something began pacing from side to side along the camp, just inside the tree line. Branches were breaking on the left side of the tent, then behind the tent, then back to the left side, and again behind the tent. Every few minutes, the sounds would cease, and the woods would go silent, only to repeat minutes later. This went on for hours. Whatever was in the woods with Joe was getting closer and closer, bolder and bolder, louder and louder.

Joe's fear took over, and he sheltered inside his tent in a desperate attempt to separate himself from the outside, even though the tent wasn't much separation at all. Joe would occasionally step outside for a moment to add a log to the fire and then go right back inside, but he noticed something unusual. He heard the footsteps moving closer to his camp while he was in his tent, then they would retreat when he left the tent. This continued like clockwork.

As his nerves ran high and fatigue set in, he finally screamed out into the night air, "Hey, bear! Hey, bear! Hey bear!" Silence responded.

All he could think to do was keep the fire burning to make it through the night. Like the previous night, however, when he went back inside his tent, small rocks started hitting the tent. One by one . . . plink . . .

plink. This confirmed in Joe's mind that whoever, or whatever, was here last night was back.

Joe started to gameplan how he could get out of the woods, but it was the middle of the night. There was no easy way out. No roads nearby, he was deep in the backcountry, and it took him a three-hour paddle and a hike through tough terrain to get out there. Taking that trip in the middle of the night would be a nightmare. Of course, at this point, which nightmare was worse? His only realistic option was to wait it out until the morning. As the sounds continued getting closer and closer and bigger and bigger, it was clear he might not make it to the morning.

It was after 3 a.m., and Joe sat inside his tent. Scared. Trembling. Unsure of the unknown in the woods around him. The sounds weren't going away. Tree knocks, branches breaking, something large pacing in the woods only twenty or thirty feet from his tent buried in the thick brush. Whatever it was, it wanted Joe to know it was there. More tiny rocks continued to hit Joe's tent. Finally in a fed-up, fear-driven panic, he yelled outside his tent.

"Leave me alone! Go away!"

Then all hell broke loose.

Suddenly he was hit with a roaring scream, so loud and powerful he could feel it in his chest. A seemingly endless scream. A frightening sound that started out guttural, like a lion's roar, and ended high-pitched, like a woman's scream in one single breath. A sound that froze Joe with fear.

It screamed repeatedly. This was no Adirondack black bear. Completely terrified beyond understanding, Joe couldn't move from his tent. His limbs wouldn't budge. He'd never experienced such dread and fear. He had no way to defend himself inside the tent or out, so his only defense was hoping this thing, this animal, this creature, would go away on its own. The roaring screams continued as Joe trembled in his tent with his eyes closed.

Branches continued to be torn down on every side of his tent. The movement and pacing were fast and big. Moving back and forth around his tent and breaking everything in its path. Like a freight train plowing through the woods.

Suddenly, as quickly as the screaming began, it stopped. Silence returned, and the quiet sounds of the river filled the forest. Joe sat motionless in his tent, paralyzed with fear. After ten minutes of silence, he muscled up the courage to look outside his tent. Slowly, he unzipped the tent and stepped out. Just then, a basketball-sized boulder came flying from the dark tree line, landing a foot away from Joe's feet. It was at this moment Joe locked in on a set of glowing red eyes staring back at him through the brush. The dark figure was as wide as a refrigerator and towered over the small evergreen trees. Petrified with fear, Joe couldn't move, yet he also couldn't look away. The glowing red eyes continued to stare him down. They were so bright that no eye shine from the flame could ever compare. Knowing the power that it took to throw a rock of this magnitude, Joe thought his life was over.

In the distance, the sounds of the predawn loon started to cry to the west. Dawn was approaching, and as the loons cried for the second time, the red eyes vanished, and the heavy footsteps disappeared into the woods. The screaming died, and the woods went quiet. Moments later, Joe worked up the courage to jump back inside his tent, where he sat trembling and praying for daylight. The loons continued to cry, and within thirty minutes, first light arrived. Joe remained in his tent for another hour waiting out the chaos and hoping whatever he saw wasn't coming back. Hoping his terrifying night was over.

After 6 a.m., Joe nervously unzipped his tent and cautiously looked around the campsite. His fire had turned to ash, and the basketball-sized boulder sat to his right. "I'm out of here," Joe thought, as he quickly started to pack up his tent and gear. When he brought his gear down to his kayak along the river, something big caught his eye: a giant footprint in the mud. Perfectly indented in the wet soil. A print that was not there last night. It was the shape of a human's foot, with toes, yet the big toe was multiple inches longer than the rest. The print measured twenty inches long. Joe knew it was time to leave, now.

Joe kept telling himself, "Maybe it's a bear print," though he knew that something more lurked in those woods, and something more than a bear was in his campsite. What frightened Joe the most was that all the noise came from the opposite side of his tent. Nowhere near the kayak or the river along his campsite.

Was this thing walking around his campsite only feet from his tent? Was there more than one of them? The sounds and screams came from the other side of the camp, yet the footprint was on the other side. So many questions arose in his mind as fear continued to fill his body, and he quickly threw his gear in the boat and started paddling. He wasn't staying another minute.

He paddled back on the Sacandaga River through the slight rapids and calm stretches, past the beaver dams and rocky carries. It was a quiet paddle, somber even. Joe stared at the shoreline, jumping at every small sound or movement. Cautiously moving through the Adirondack wilderness he'd spent his whole life wandering. This rugged land felt different now. It was a wild place he didn't know as well as he thought he did. A place where something large and terrifying wandered in clear sight. A place that was home to secrets he couldn't explain. A place he no longer recognized, and that is what truly scared Joe the most.

We may never know exactly what Joe encountered those June nights, lurking deep in the most remote parts of the Adirondack Park. The powerful tree knocks; the giant, shadowy figure; the screams; the glowing red eyes in the darkness. But we do know one thing: He'll think twice before he ever paddles back into those once-familiar now unrecognizable woods along the Sacandaga River. And he'll never go camping alone ever again.

CHAPTER FIVE

THE GHOST TOWN OF ADIRONDAC

Diana Gallagher and James Appleton

Deep in the wilderness of the Adirondack Mountains, many secrets remain hidden just beyond the evergreens. Places where history can be relived. Where the old settlers of the past are alive and well. Whether it's old-time logging roads, iconic villages, lojs and hotels, old iron furnaces, or abandoned railroad tracks laid more than a century ago, history lives in this rugged land. But beyond that, if you go just a little farther through the trees, you'll find something much more forgotten. Places that remain hidden behind the spruce grove. But be careful. If you take one step too far to the right, you'll miss it. Never even knowing it was there behind those branches. Forgotten villages where its citizens remain intact. Where time stands still. Ghost towns hidden in plain sight. For Eve, a weekend adventure to the mountains slowly turned into something much more than she bargained for. Where following the wrong path led her into the forgotten iron past of the Adirondacks. A mysterious trail deep in the woods that led her straight into the ghost town known as Adirondac.

September. Crisp nights and crunching leaves, morning fog lining the lakes and rivers. Having spent many summer weekends hiking through the High Peaks, Eve knew how quickly the seasons would evaporate in the Adirondacks. So on a cloudless Friday morning, she tossed her hiking gear and camera into her car and drove out of the busy city of Brooklyn, New York, away from the honks, the sirens, and all the people. Sure, she hadn't slept much for the past two weeks, but she couldn't resist the call of a bluebird weekend with only a slight chance of rain showers up in the ADK.

Over the bridges, through the tunnels, and up the highway she went, leaving the bustling big city behind and heading due north for a weekend wilderness adventure. As she drove down the familiar road to Upper Works, the distinctive gray stone tower emerged through the yellow and orange leaves. The MacIntyre Iron Furnace. Of course, Eve had heard about the historic towns of Adirondac and Tahawus that it represented, with the furnace serving as the tallest relic of their mining history. Eve decided on this trip that she would take the time to explore it properly. After all, she was here, right? She might as well take advantage of it.

She pulled over and parked the car, and the distant, soothing tumble of the Hudson River filled the air. Shouldering her camera, she locked the car and left her backpack behind. She'd only be there for a few minutes, after all.

Eve read the informational signs, noting the area's origin as first the village of Adirondac, until the town's abandonment in 1857. Later, it was reclaimed as Tahawus—first as a fish-and-game club and later as a titanium-mining site in World War II. But eventually, the forest reclaimed this town. Nature reigned supreme, as it always does.

She hiked past the furnace, sidestepping the signs that cautioned staying on the path. Crunching through the underbrush, she observed remnants of the past tucked away with the fallen leaves, a rusted twist of metal here, an old rock wall there.

At first, the lighting was ideal, so Eve picked up her camera, framing the blazing red leaves against the gray sky. But the wind rose, scattering branches, and soon, charcoal storm clouds raced overhead as a cool autumn breeze blew through the forest. She shivered, pulling her fleece closer. "Just a little farther," she thought.

A few steps later, Eve spotted a small, lone cairn positioned between two large spruce trees. As she approached it, she felt a blast of heat, as though from an open oven. Suddenly, she found herself sweating. "Well, that's strange," she thought, fanning herself with her hands.

Eve followed what she figured to be the path behind the cairn, although it had long since been overtaken by tangled grass and fallen leaves. In the dying light, the shadows began to look the same. But just as she considered turning around, there stood a second cairn, resting on the crumbling brick remnants of what looked to be a fireplace up ahead. Curiously, she continued up the old trail, noticing her skin blazing as she approached the cairn, only to immediately cool off once she passed it. "Hmm, probably something to do with the old furnace," she thought, ignoring the unusual chill running down her spine.

A third cairn rested on a gnarled pile of metal. As Eve stepped toward it, the warmth returned, her skin prickled, and her breathing hitched. Then, the forest went still.

She knew it instinctively: She was no longer alone in the woods. "Hello? Hello?" she nervously called out into the evergreens.

At once, three men strode through the undergrowth. Eve jumped aside, startled. This was a popular hiking area, after all. Unlike her hiking gear, however, they wore soot-covered overalls and jaunty caps, lugging metal pails and pickaxes.

She let out a surprised laugh. "Hey, sorry—"

The men breezed right past her as if she didn't exist.

"Wow. Rude much?" she said out loud. She wasn't surprised with this behavior, though; she was a New Yorker, after all.

"Like I was sayin'," one of the soot-covered men said. "There's better work to be had down in the city."

The second man shuddered. "Who needs all of that lot when you have this?" The man raised both arms, motioning to grand wilderness surrounding them.

"My cousin wrote me a letter saying they're planning a park," the first man continued, undeterred. "Supposed to be the biggest one in the city."

"A letter," Eve thought. "How quaint." She racked her brain, wondering what the man meant by a planned park. Surely there weren't any square inches left on the island of Manhattan. She opened her mouth to ask, but the men had vanished into the shadows beyond the cairn.

Confused but writing it off as an odd group of outdoorsmen, Eve took another step to her right and noticed a patch of light glowed beyond the trees, and she carefully picked her way toward it. Beneath her feet, the green grass began to mat down. The old, crumbled brick fireplaces alongside her righted themselves, growing taller and sturdier, as if they were brand new.

Eve moved through the branches toward the light, where she landed on a dirt path, and suddenly a bustling village spread before her eyes. Lining both sides of the dirt road were tidy rows of identical cottages with two cracked windows apiece. In the center, a church hunched with a sagging roof, its splintered steeple rising toward the dark sky. In front of her, a large, white clapboard building with rows of broken windowpanes watched her. But when she looked closer, the fractures in the glass appeared to heal. The overgrown gardens swiftly blossomed into shades of pastel. She turned her head, and the church, too, seemed to stand taller, its steeple becoming whole and proud. *Creeeeeak.* Down by the river, a water wheel groaned to life, methodically churning water.

Clang. Sparks flew from the furnace, tall and austere, like a Mayan pyramid even in the darkness. Eve watched, fascinated, as a crew of men carted supplies across a wooden trestle to the top of the furnace, silhouetted by the glowing tangerine light. They shouted out to a group below, who positioned themselves around the stone archway. As if on a signal, the men fed the furnace in a carefully choreographed dance, prodding the ovens with a long iron pole, and the blaze roared so loudly that she covered her ears.

Turning away, Eve spotted a small boy in torn pants and a dusty white shirt holding out a stick to a slender gray dog. "Oh, hello," she said with a smile, squatting down to meet the boy's height. "What's going on here?"

The boy stood still. The dog's ears swiveled forward. But then the boy waved at the air, as if troubled by a mosquito, and resumed his game of tug of war.

Straightening up, Eve was startled to realize she recognized the building in front of her: the MacNaughton Cottage. Except instead of being midrenovation, it looked freshly painted, and smoke rose from its chimney. The single-story right wing had a sign that read, "BANK." Eve stood staring at the bank sign, pondering where she had wandered to. Where did these woods take her?

Moments later, a glimmer lying on the ground in front of the white building caught Eve's eye. She walked over and picked up two shining silver coins reflecting the afternoon sunlight. Surrounded by engraved, twisting corn, the back of the coins read "HALF DIME." She flipped them over to discover a raised Lady Liberty seated with a flag and gazing off at the precise dotted edges circling the coin's diameter. At the bottom was the year: 1855.

"I must be sleeping," she decided, dropping the coins into her pocket. "This is all an elaborate dream." Eve was sure that she was back in Williamsburg, and soon she'd resurface to the whine of traffic and the rumble of the G train.

But the morning seemed reluctant to arrive, so she picked up her camera and took photos of the teenage girls chatting on the church steps across the street from the bank, the wind billowing their long, floral-patterned dresses. Of the horse trotting down the dirt road, its tail whisking from side to side, and of the rider tipping his cap to the girls, causing them to giggle. Then she took more photos of the cottages, candlelight flickering in their windows as shadows moved from pane to pane. Of the fire, standing in stark contrast to the inky night sky. No matter how far she walked, the furnace stayed visible like a beacon, the heat palpable no matter the gusty winds. The longer she walked, the more the town began to take on a shimmer from the heat.

The church bells rang out, marking the hour, but she lost count. With her mind in awe, and her legs moving on autopilot, Eve wandered past the blacksmith's shop and over the wooden train tracks cut into the earth. She listened to the grind of the gristmill and the tumbling water of the dark river beyond. Soon, the water drowned out every other sound.

The river lapped against her shoes, and its wet chill snapped her back to reality. At that moment, the feeling in the air changed, and anxiety filled her stomach. Without understanding why, she suddenly knew that it was time to go. Something bad was coming.

But go where? Where was she? How did she get to this town? What is this town? Where is her car? Eve's mind raced with unanswered questions.

In the village center, everything stopped on a dime—the horse and its rider, the girls on the steps, the boy and his dog. The church bells halted. In the silence that followed, a long, low groaning filled the air. Then everyone began to run.

"FIRE!"

Eve braced herself, expecting the collision of bones and muscle, but instead the bodies whisked past her like storm clouds as if she wasn't there. Hooves thundered by, spraying mud up onto her.

From the top of the furnace, the tightly packed bricks exploded, raining down fireballs into the street. The wooden trestle splintered and tumbled over itself. Molten ore gushed through the archway and flooded the gardens. Screams and shouts rose all around her as doors slammed open and shut.

Eve raced over to the boardinghouse door. "Help!" she shouted. She tried to knock, but her fist couldn't connect with the wood. She couldn't make a sound. Eve knew she had to get out of there, and she had to get out of there now.

Sprinting down the dirt road, she ducked behind a wagon. In the distance, chickens squawked in panic, and terrified voices called out in the chaos. With a sickening crack, the church caved in on itself, the steeple crashing to the ground where Eve had stood moments before. Then the wind whipped the sparks into the wagon, and it went up in flames. She scrambled backwards as her vision exploded with blazing white.

In the roaring light, something caught her eye once again. There, by the tree line, was a lone cairn. Eve stood up and ran toward it. But the faster she moved, the closer the fire pursued her. Blasts of stifling, choking-hot air caused her eyes to tear as she slipped on wet leaves and crashed over stone foundations. More buildings caught fire and collapsed to the ground in front of her. Eve's breath was short and came in ragged gasps. She sprinted toward the trees and turned around—and there was the village, engulfed in the inferno.

In front of her, leaping flames burned her eyes. Behind her, the dense, dark forest remained, refusing to give up its secrets. How was she supposed to get back?

"Think, Eve, think!" her mind screamed.

With shaking hands, she hastily picked up her camera and zoomed in deep through the trees. *Click.* For a brief instant, the white flash illuminated the forest. There it was—the trail and the second cairn.

As she took off toward the cairn, fog seeped through the forest, whispering and wrapping around the trees. It momentarily dulled the sound of the turmoil behind her. With every deep breath, she coughed. The fog tasted like smoke.

The farther she ran, the thicker the fog grew and the hotter the temperature rose as she searched in vain for the third cairn. The one that would free her from this nightmare. But there was no sign of it. Only the raging flames chasing closer and closer, snapping tree trunks and scorching branches in their wake, rising, and weaving in the distorted light. A burning sensation shot up her shoulder, and she screamed.

Finally, she busted out of the tree line and her feet struck the cracked pavement of the road—

The fire vanished.

The fog receded, as though it had been sucked away by a vacuum.

The night quieted.

The flames were gone. The screams were gone. Only the sounds of crickets and the river remained.

"What just happened?"

Eve stumbled into her car and sped up the road to Upper Works trailhead. Dazed and disoriented, she couldn't make herself exit the car. Instead, she locked the doors and curled up in the driver's seat, where she sat for the night, scared, confused, and in disbelief of what she just experienced.

"Where is the fire?" she thought to herself. Eve eventually fell asleep from shock and exhaustion in the front seat of her car. Hours later, she woke to sunlight streaming through the windows. Birds chirped as a soft breeze sighed through the branches. All around her, car doors slammed shut as fellow hikers shouldered their gear for a day on the trail.

Eve exhaled with relief. "Man," she thought, "what a weird dream." Time traveling? Furnace fires? Old mining towns? It had all felt so realistic, but she felt it was a sign that she probably should've had more for dinner yesterday than just a Stewart's milkshake. She gathered her backpack, strapped on her camera, and locked her car door. She wouldn't let the remnants of a strange dream throw off the rest of this weekend in the woods.

Just then, a group of hikers walked past her car. Eve rolled down her window and asked, "Hey, did you hear about a forest fire of some kind around here last night?"

The hikers were surprised by the question and responded simply, "No," giving Eve the confirmation that it must have been a bizarre dream at the trailhead.

Eve snapped a few quick photos as she stepped onto the trail. Then she followed a small group of hikers ahead of her. Out of character but for good reason, she no longer wanted to hike alone today.

As she picked up her pace to catch up with the hikers, she heard jingling in her pocket. She reached inside and pulled out two coins that were so rusted she had to stop to examine them. "They were probably change from a Metrocard machine long ago," she told herself. Except her mind flashed back to the half-dimes she'd picked up in her dream. Was it a dream, though? The longer she looked, the more the brown lump in the center of the coins resembled the seated Lady Liberty . . .

She balled her hand into a fist. She *really* needed to catch up on sleep. But as Eve dropped the coins back into her pocket, her eyes caught the scorched fabric on the sleeve of her fleece jacket.

"No way," she thought. Blood rushed in her ears as she stood frozen in the middle of the trail, her mind running through every possible explanation.

Except there weren't any. At least, not any rational ones.

That was just a dream. There was no way that was real.

Right?

Eve remembered her camera. With shaking hands, she clicked through the photos. There were the images she'd taken of the foliage, the rest stop, the "Welcome to the Adirondacks" sign, the river. But the photos of the village, the teenage girls in floral dresses, the horse, the boy and his dog, the gristmill—gone. The camera roll jumped thirteen numbers, from image 62 to image 75, landing on the picture she'd just taken moments ago outside her car.

The rest of those photos, like the village itself, had managed to disappear. But where did they go? Eve may never know what truly happened in the woods that evening. She may never know how she got to that old ghost town. But she will certainly be wary of following an unknown cairn the next time she finds herself in search of a weekend adventure in the Adirondack Park.

So if you find yourself roaming around the MacIntyre Iron Furnace as night falls, take heed. If you follow the cairns, you may just discover that the ghost town of Adirondac is very much alive and well.

The ghost towns of Adirondac and Tahawus are out there. Hidden just beyond the evergreens. A secret world nestled in the woods of the MacIntyre Iron Furnace. But where are the cairns leading travelers back to the forgotten places of this rugged wilderness? That's the mystery. A mystery Eve would prefer to leave behind her. Just be careful the next time you're out in the woods. You never know where those cairns you're following might take you. You may just find yourself walking back in time to the days of old in the Adirondack Park.

CHAPTER SIX

THE CURSE OF THE FLOATING LOGS

The floating logs. A warzone stretch of trail deep in the High Peaks Wilderness. A swampy mess lined with downed trees and free-floating logs serving as footbridges across the mucky chaos. A trail notorious for ruining hikers' days. But maybe something else stalks that land. Maybe something else causes the disarray that surrounds the floating logs. Something sinister in the wood line or maybe under the water. Whatever it is, you'll know when it sees you. By the time you see it, though, it's too late. For John, a meticulously planned trip into the Adirondack backcountry would be completly erased when he made one small mistake. Because if you dare challenge this land, you will lose.

The leaves were changing, and that meant one thing: time to get to the Adirondacks. With unmatched fall foliage, there was no better place to take in the colorful majestic views than from the highest point in the state, Mount Marcy. John decided it was now or never to head up to the ADK for a weekend adventure. As a Buffalo native, he had visited the park a few times throughout his life, and because he recently took up hiking, climbing the tallest peak in the state was on top of his bucket list. This weekend was the weekend to check that off the list.

John loaded his car early Friday morning and began the trek east to the blue line. He was vigilant about doing his homework before the hike, and he had all the gear he needed. After all, he was climbing the tallest peak in the state, so he figured he should overprepare for this one. As he drove, he laid the High Peaks map out on the passenger seat for a visual, and he went through the route. "First I'll go 3.2 miles from the Loj to Marcy Dam, cross over the dam, then right onto Avalanche Pass, then left onto the Lake Arnold Trail," he repeated over and over in his head as he drove across the state.

With the beautiful weather and foliage, John was making it a full-weekend camping trip. His plan was to hike in and camp at Marcy Dam for an early-Saturday-morning start. Because he was staying at Marcy Dam, he could make a nice loop out of Mount Marcy via the Lake Arnold Trail up and back down the other side of the mountain on the Van Hoevenberg Trail, landing him right back at his campsite. A perfect plan for a great weekend in the High Peaks.

Before he knew it, John was crossing into the Adirondack Park, marked by the brown and yellow sign, "Now entering Adirondack Park." A sign that boasts a magical yet mysterious quality. The drive through the park along Route 3 feels never ending, but this time of year, it was magnificent. Colorful trees filled the landscape as the sunshine lit up the blue sky. A truly picturesque start to his trip.

The weather was supposed to be flawless this weekend, with no signs of rain. John, however, was prepared for the worst anyways and still had his rain jacket. With a couple hours left in his drive, he made a pit stop at Stewart's just before Star Lake to fuel up and get a few additional treats for the weekend's adventure. Beef jerky, peanuts, and some extra candy bars. The essentials.

"Going hiking?" the cashier asked enthusiastically.

"I am, yes!" John replied. "I'm heading up Mount Marcy."

The cashier's tone immediately changed as she looked nervously at the newspaper rack across the store. "Well, just make sure you always look behind you out there."

Confused and noticing her uneasiness, John shrugged it off, grabbed his snacks, and headed for the door. As he was walking out, the newspaper rack caught his eye. On the front page was a photo of an Adirondack lean-to with the headline "Another Weekend, Another Hiker Missing in the High Peaks." John picked up the paper and examined it closer for a moment before heading back to his car.

John opened the bed of his truck, where he laid out his backpack and began loading his snacks. While he was placing his treats into the bear cannister, he overhead a local man in a green flannel shirt at the gas pump talking to another man. "No, they haven't found any of them yet. They probably just keep getting lost and eaten by Bigfoot," one joked.

The other pointed at John and said playfully, "This guy will probably be next!"

With this being John's first big hiking outing and his first time climbing solo, he didn't want to put those images into his head, so he playfully laughed and quickly brushed off the man's comments. He finished loading his backpack before hopping into his truck.

He arrived at Lake Placid midafternoon with plenty of time to hike the 3.2 miles into Marcy Dam and get set up for the night of camping, another first for John. Because he was a researcher and a planner, John had everything he needed for the trip: tent, sleeping bag, sleeping pad, cookware, and freeze-dried meals. He was prepared and set for the adventure. He pulled into the Adirondack Loj trailhead and was immediately hit with the smell of that fresh mountain air. After getting his gear together, he suited up with his fully loaded backpack, locked his car, and stepped up to the trailhead registry to sign in. John noticed several "Missing Hiker" signs posted at the trailhead. Three hikers had gone missing in the last few weeks. John grew nervous, and he contemplated whether he really wanted to tackle this adventure alone. Having made the long drive from Buffalo and doing his homework before the hike, John decided now was the time. After all, he prepared himself for the hike. Despite the uneasiness, he set off. The adventure was underway!

Having studied the map and read all the online forums, John couldn't believe he was finally here as he traversed the trail toward Marcy Dam, passing the very signs and junctions he studied on the map for weeks. The weather was perfect: seventy degrees and sunny with the foliage near peak. On the hike to the dam where John would camp for the night, he didn't pass a single other hiker, which surprised him, given the time of year and weather. No matter, he was ready for a solo weekend in the great outdoors.

He soon made it to Marcy Dam, where the destroyed footbridge he'd seen many photos of awaited him. Yellow, orange, and red leaves lit up the mountain landscape, while the crystal-clear Marcy Brook rushed under his feet. In awe of the views of Wright Peak, Mount Colden, and Whales Tail, John thought to himself, "This was the right decision this weekend."

Having arrived at his destination for the night, John eagerly crossed over the wooden footbridge to the east side of Marcy Brook, where he quickly found an empty campsite for the weekend. In anticipation of this weekend's camping trip, John had pitched his tent dozens of times in his living room, so he had his camp set up in under two minutes.

After laying out his sleeping bag in his tent, John overheard some talking through the woods and noticed a vacant lean-to across the trail. Excited to converse with fellow hikers, he went and said hello. The two campers at the lean-to were rather disheveled and told John they were friends of one of the missing hikers.

"And that's the last anyone heard from him. We've been out here searching for the past five days," one camper said as he changed into a fresh shirt that certainly did not smell fresh.

"Something weird is going on in these woods," the other man said from inside the lean-to. "Three weekends in a row, someone has gone missing. All of them climbing Mount Marcy."

John's nerves were now on even higher alert as he left the two men's campsite and went back to his tent.

The sun was beginning to set, so John grabbed his headlamp and walked down to the brook to take in the sunset as the golden-hour light shined over Mount Colden. Despite his raised nerves as the darkness filled the Adirondack woods, John went to sleep early so he could wake up early and begin his climb up Mount Marcy.

The next morning, John enjoyed a quick breakfast outside his tent before filling up his water bottles at the brook. It was time to hike, and he was antsy to start moving, so he grabbed his backpack and started on the trail. He planned to loop up and over Mount Marcy, ending back at his tent at Marcy Dam, so up Avalanche Pass he went. The sun was shining, the birds were singing, and the woods were more colorful than a rainbow. John couldn't ask for better conditions as his nerves about the missing hikers subsided. He continued along Avalanche Pass as the roaring Marcy Brook flowed past him on his right. It wasn't long until John passed over a footbridge across the Marcy Brook, landing him at the trail junction he was looking for, the beginning of the Lake Arnold Trail, which would take him to the base of Mount Marcy at Feldspar Brook.

As he approached the Avalanche Pass campsite, he saw a couple people but not who he expected to see. Two forest rangers, Ranger Scott and Ranger Thomas, were in the middle of taking down a tent and piling up some camping gear. "Hey, good morning!" John said with a smile.

The rangers were focused on the task at hand and didn't hear John walking up the trail. "Oh, hey there, nice day today," Ranger Scott responded.

"You guys even camp out here while you're working?" John innocently asked.

"No, actually," Ranger Thomas responded, "this is the camping gear from a missing hiker. Have you heard about what's been going on lately?"

John told the rangers he had heard about a missing hiker, but he didn't know much more. What they told him next sent shivers down his spine.

"Well, someone has gone missing every Saturday for the past five weeks in a row," Ranger Scott informed him. "Today is Saturday. Something strange is going on in the High Peaks."

The rangers handed John a "Missing Hiker" flyer with photos and descriptions of each hiker and urged him to be on the lookout for any of them or anything unusual in the woods. John looked over the images of the five strangers.

"A lot of red backpacks," he said to the rangers as he scanned the flyer.

"Yeah, maybe the mountains are tired of red," Ranger Scott sarcastically responded.

They said their goodbyes, and John continued his journey toward Mount Marcy, slightly shaken by the new information because one or two missing hikers could be a tragic coincidence, but five hikers consistently seven days apart felt a bit more malevolent.

He traversed the Lake Arnold Trail, slowly and steadily climbing along the eastern flanks of Mount Colden toward the small backcountry pond known as Lake Arnold. The air was fresh, the wind was nonexistent, and the temperatures were in the low sixties with expected highs in the low seventies. A scenic bluebird Adirondack day, but despite the sunshine, the flowing river streams, and the colorful mountain landscape, John felt restless as he continued to think about the five missing hikers. Five people felt too extreme to be coincidence or the typical unprepared-hiker tragedy he read so much about during his research. "How would that many people just vanish?" he thought to himself. "Was it something that got them, or was it someone?" Both possibilities were unsettling, and neither seemed better than the other.

His climb continued past Lake Arnold before skirting between Mount Colden to the west on his right and Mount Marcy on his left to the east. Still no sign of any other hikers out on the trail that day, which would have relieved his nerves. Moments later, John arrived at a stretch of trail he had read about, a warzone-like area of downed trees and swampy, mucky water known to Adirondack hikers as the "floating logs."

A one-hundred-yard stretch notorious for ruining hikers' days with everything from drenched boots to full-on plunges in the water, soaking them head to toe in its brown, murky water. Wooden logs and planks floated aimlessly atop the water, while dead trees lined the bottom, with branches like daggers waiting to impale a hiker who falls in, some partially attached to the ground, others free-floating to be used like a raft by the hikers who dared cross. The water sat just a foot or two deep in some places and as much as five feet deep in others. So when John arrived, he cautiously began planning his route across.

Sadly, there was no obvious route to the other side. The more he looked around, the more desolate this remote land felt. It seemed like no human had ever even been back here, let alone thousands of hikers for decades. Before beginning the journey across the logs, John instinctively loosened his shoulder straps and unclipped the chest and waist straps from his backpack. This way, if he fell into the boggy swamp, he could quickly detach his backpack and not risk his biggest fear: drowning.

John began the trek across, gently auditioning the first log with his foot before slowly adding more and more weight until it stopped sinking. The first log only sunk a few inches into the water, covering the top of John's waterproof boots just below the shoelaces. A good start for John as he shimmied his way along the log into the depths of the water and farther from solid ground. Using his trekking poles to balance, he slowly yet methodically took one step at a time, the log slowly sinking with every shift of his weight. He made it to the end of the first log and stepped to the next one, which was floating at an angle heading toward a small patch of land. He started to assess to the second log now, testing his weight before fully committing, when suddenly a large hurricane-like gust of wind ripped through the area, violently shaking the trees around the forest and throwing John off balance as his body shifted from side to side trying to regain control.

John had no choice now but to commit to the next log and pray it would hold him. He lunged forward, landing directly in the middle of the log, which immediately sank up to John's ankle, just above his boot. With no time to think, John instinctively launched himself into the air again toward the small patch of land and quickly grabbed onto a tree to reel himself in. Due to John's quick response, he avoided a boot entirely full of water but still had a slightly wet boot and sock.

Now, as he stood in the middle of this swampy bog, he planned the next part of his journey across the logs. This area, however, had a strange feeling to it, one that John couldn't figure out. The woods felt different here, but he didn't know why. He felt as if he was being watched as he moved about the fallen trees floating throughout the water. John's eyes scanned the tree line, unsure what he was looking for, perhaps someone watching him or maybe a sign of a missing hiker. The woods didn't reveal anything unusual, so John shifted his eyes back onto the next challenge: continuing across the logs.

The edges were lined with thick, green spruce trees and peppered with colorful hardwoods. The feeling of being watched became harder to shake as he continued to game-plan his next moves. He became increasingly unable to focus on the task at hand, and his eyes kept moving back to the tree line on the edge of the swamp. The air was noticeably colder here. Navigating terrain that was far above John's experience level, his nerves were at an all-time high. Observing the tree line, John started to see a path reveal itself. He had one more wet area to cross where a series of dry wooden planks lined the trail. "Perfect!" he thought to himself. He stepped to the other side of the tree he was holding onto and walked along the edge of the water to the next and final log.

This final log was attached with an old nail on one end and free floating on the other, but it was the only way to get across the swamp. He stepped up onto the final log and slowly began sidestepping across it. Slow and steady, he shuffled a half-step at a time, hunched over to keep his center of gravity as low as possible. Every step was a test of his balance. Instinctively, John used his trekking poles to guide the free-floating end of the log to his destination, pushing against both the ground and other trees in the water. This technique was working, and the log was moving directly where he needed to land.

As the makeshift raft pointed John in the right direction, something else caught his eye, reflecting the sunlight underneath the water. It was a set of car keys on a bright red carabiner. Wondering if these keys were a past hiker's stroke of bad luck or a clue to help the authorities with the string of the recent missing hikers, John braced himself on the log, and using his trekking pole as an extension of his hands, he reached in the water and carefully hooked the red carabiner.

While John was fishing for car keys, he saw something staring at him from underneath the water—a frog. The frog's eyes were locked on John's, as if staring into the depths of his soul. Time froze, and John and the aquatic creature shared a moment, one that gave John a feeling of uneasiness. Just then, another heavy gust blew through the swamp, breaking John's moment with the amphibian and his balance, as the trees thrashed around him and the wind sent ripples into the water. He stood up, desperately trying to restore his balance, but unable to, he stepped off the log with his right foot and into the water. Wet and frustrated, John stood half in the swamp, half straddling the log. His left leg sank into the mucky water up to his thigh, and his right leg, bent at the knee, still stood atop the floating log.

John's attention to the car keys and the frog in the water was now turned to getting back up on the log and out of the swamp. Using the strength of his dry leg and his trekking poles, he began hoisting himself back up onto the log. But when he tried to step up, he couldn't move. His foot wouldn't budge. Maybe it was stuck in the muck, or maybe it was wedged under some deadfall. It felt as though his boot was being held underneath the water. He kept tugging and eventually freed his boot and climbed back onto the log. Without any hesitation and with one boot already soaked, John launched himself off the log onto the dry land, finally completing his first trip across the floating logs.

"Well, that was stupid," John said to himself. He looked back at the swamp as he stood on the plank boardwalk.

Because the worst was over, John swapped out his wet sock for a fresh one. "Good as new," he proudly said to himself as he attached the wet sock to his backpack to dry in the fresh, sunny mountain air. He continued his hike and moments later arrived at Feldspar Brook and the junction for the Mount Marcy Trail. Another destination checked off the list as he continued to go through the map in his head.

He had roughly two thousand feet of elevation gain over two miles to the summit ahead of him, so the hard work was just beginning. However, the sun was shining, the foliage was stunning, and the memory of the hellish time across the floating logs was quickly fading from his memory as the High Peak's views started to reveal themselves through the trees. John began marking checkpoints off his list as he climbed the trail along Feldspar Brook, nestled between Gray Peak and Mount Skylight. Gray Trail junction, check; Lake Tear of the Clouds, check; the Four Corners, check.

John made terrific time scaling the trail to the Four Corners, which was the final trail junction he needed to hit before the final push up Mount Marcy. His morale was high now, as he could start to see the summit above him, towering in the sky, mightier than any skyscraper. He fueled up with a quick snack before leaving the tree line for the final quarter-mile of climbing on the exposed rock. He moved quickly with excitement, confidence, and pride as he traveled from rock cairn to cairn.

And then he arrived. The summit of Mount Marcy. He had officially climbed the tallest mountain in the state. Brimming with joy, he snapped some photos of the magnificent landscape. The 360-degree views felt like they went to the end of the globe.

"Time for lunch!" John declared, a lunch well earned. After all, he survived the infamous floating logs and made it up the tallest peak in the state. An accomplishment for even the most experienced of hikers. He found a ledge to sit on and enjoy some chips and a summit sandwich, and he conversed with fellow hikers who, like John, were from western New York.

"What a perfect view! Thank God we made it, though, am I right?" the man said to John, as he switched out of a drenched-with-sweat blue Buffalo Bills hat for a dry red Buffalo Bills hat. "We almost canceled our trip this weekend."

Continuing to take in the stunning views, John politely asked, "Oh, why did you almost cancel your trip?"

"Because of all of the hikers going missing," the man responded. "Something bizarre is happening in these woods, if you ask me." The man snapped some more photos with his cell phone.

"Yeah, I've heard about that. It's unsettling," John admitted.

"Each of them was hiking Mount Marcy, too, which makes it even weirder," the man said.

"Oh, I didn't know that little fact. Yikes!" John responded as his nerves started to return.

"Yeah, that's why we came up the Van Hoevenberg Trail because they were all climbing from the other side of the mountain."

This information put John on high alert because he came up from the other side of the mountain.

"I don't know what's happening out there," the man in the hat continued, "but I don't want to run into whoever or whatever is out there."

John finished his lunch and said goodbye to the man, who playfully wished John good luck on his climb down. John was planning to descend the Van Hoevenberg Trail to make a loop out of the mountain back to his campsite at Marcy Dam, but now knowing all five people went missing while hiking up the trail he just successfully climbed, John felt like he had to go back. He had to be more vigilant and look for some clues to help find information on any of these missing people.

He changed his plans and dropped off the summit from the same direction he arrived. He followed the cairns back down to the tree line, where he went over Schofield Cobble, back to the Four Corners. As he descended the mountain, he was staring off in every direction, looking for anything unusual. He also started to wonder if that was why he didn't see a single other hiker all day until he arrived on the summit. His nerves were high again and the woods felt darker to him. Menacing. He followed Feldspar Brook down the mountain and was back at the Lake Arnold Trail junction, the trail he came in on. No sign of anyone or anything unusual so far.

He turned right and began walking back along the Lake Arnold Trail. It now occurred to John that his well-intentioned decision to play detective sadly meant another go around with the floating logs, a moment of realization that was not met with enthusiasm. As he approached the wooden boardwalk that led him to the floating logs, the woods began to feel different. They felt dark. The wind started to blow through the mountains, and the sound of falling leaves and swaying trees filled the air. John stopped in his tracks and examined the woods because suddenly things felt off. The air was different. The hair on the back of his neck stood up. Unsure if this was his mind playing tricks on him or if something, or someone, was in the woods with him, John clutched his trekking poles tighter and continued moving forward along the wooden planks.

He arrived at the swamp, where the logs floated in a completely different maze from before. It was time to cross, despite feeling unexplainable dread. The woods were off, and he knew it. He wanted to get out of this area quickly. Before crossing, John took off his backpack to put the now-dry sock from earlier inside this pack. This way, if he dunked again, he could change into dry socks. Once again, he felt like he was being watched. In a rush, he put on his pack, clipped his waist and chest straps, and started to cross the water.

With his trekking pole, he pulled a log close to the land's edge and started walking on it, hovering over the water. Without incident, he made his way back onto the small patch of land. John's nerves were growing as he kept looking at the tree line, waiting for something to come out of it. His heart was beating faster as the wind continued to howl. The trees rattled all over the forest, and John planned his next step across the deeper water. He began walking on top of a second log, slow and steady, while balancing himself with his trekking poles.

Suddenly, something caught his eye under the water. It was a back-pack buried in mud and blowdown. John examined it for a moment, looking through the mucky ripples. It was dark in color, with silver zippers reflecting off the sunlight. John stood on the log, floating over the backpack, and wondered if this could be the clue he was looking for. John then noticed something else in the water. It was a frog staring at him once again. The two locked eyes before *SNAP!*

The log John stood on suddenly split in half, dropping him into the middle of the swamp. He fell backward and was now fully submerged in the brown, murky water lined with fallen trees. He went to stand up but found himself caught. His pack was stuck between the blowdown and wouldn't budge. Under the water, John thrashed and pulled at his pack but couldn't gain any momentum to move.

The seconds were ticking now as his torso continued tugging in a desperate attempt to dislodge the pack from the blowdown. With no success, John went to plan B. His breath beginning to fade, he tried taking off his pack, but it was tightly secured to his body. John's worst night-mare was coming true as thoughts of drowning overtook him while he continued to violently thrash under the water, trying to get his backpack off. Miraculously, the log he was stuck against finally gave way, freeing John and his backpack.

John stood up out of the water with a giant gasp and crawled up the dry land lined with more blowdown and hardwood trees as he frantically tried to regain his breath. Breathing heavily, wet, and covered in mud, he laid down on the side of the trail to recover. A near-drowning experience in the Adirondacks was not what John anticipated for this weekend's adventure.

John was now past the logs, and at this point, there wasn't a dry inch on his body, but at least he made it across. He took a few minutes to settle down, and then the only thing on his mind was getting back to his campsite. He started walking again, but moments later, he remembered the backpack he saw in the water.

"Could that have been a missing hiker's pack?" he thought to himself. After experiencing what he did, could they have drowned in there? Unable to shake the feeling mixed with curiosity, John turned back to scope out the logs one more time and try to recover the backpack, figuring it may help the authorities locate someone.

Minutes after falling victim to the floating logs, John was back at the start, examining the swamp. He skirted his way to the edge, where he could get a glimpse in the water to see the backpack. He figured, because he was already soaked, recovering the pack wouldn't take very long. The wind began to rip through the land as the trees shook violently and the chorus of leaves sang around the woods. John scanned the water.

"Found it!" John excitedly said to himself when he located the red backpack. It was no longer buried in the water. Rather, it was floating against some blowdown. John's fall into the water must have also freed this mystery backpack. He stepped onto a log headed directly to the backpack. He walked along the log and cautiously squatted down to pick up the pack.

As he reached for it, he saw two frogs swimming next to the backpack. The wind picked up again, and when John grabbed the pack, a feeling of unexplainable dread overtook him. He felt a presence swoop in directly behind him on the log. His reflexes took over, and as he turned around, he was immediately pulled underneath the water.

Bubbles filled the water at the floating logs for the next couple minutes. The wind howled, and the trees thrashed, and then the land calmed down once again. The bubbles ceased.

Soon, a group of fresh hikers arrived at the bog and decided to bushwhack around the swamp instead of testing the logs, entirely unaware of what took place only minutes earlier at the infamous floating logs.

The floating logs. A treacherous stretch of trail occupied by something. Or maybe it is someone. What's in that water? Who's in those woods? No one really knows for sure, but you'll find out if you enter this rugged country.

If you dare cross its water. The mystery that surrounds these logs remains. Beware, if you dare to hike down this trail, you're rolling the dice on whether you'll make it back to the trailhead or not. Like John, you could do everything right when you head into the mountains; you could have all the gear, experience, and skills you need. But in the end, one wrong move is all it takes, because the mountains will always win.

CHAPTER SEVEN

THE LEGEND OF THE FAUST LUMBERJACK

←——— ≪ • ≫ ———→

October. A month that brings the haunts, ghouls, and unexplainable phenomena to life, even if just for a single night. Why would that be? What is it about October that brings the dead back to life and raises the hair on the backs of our necks as we feel a presence standing behind us? Only to look back and see . . . nothing. Could it be the orange autumn moon? Or could it be one last chance for the dead to seek vengeance on their enemies before All Hallows' Eve?

Hard to say, really. What can't be denied is that this time of year brings an uneasiness about the night. Things seen outside our windows, staring at us in the darkness through the plate glass, causing even adults to hide under their covers like children. Praying whatever lurks outside those covers can't find them. I suppose we never really outgrow those childhood instincts. After all, our homes are supposed to be where we can seek safety and refuge from the cruel world around us. But what if your home is the place that instills the most fear? What if you must seek refuge from your home? What then?

The days are short, but the nights are long this time of year. The warm, relaxing summer days are now replaced by a cool, haunting eerieness. The autumn wind scatters the leaves among the forest. Branches gently tap our windows while the wind whistles through the chilly night air. What is it about this haunted time of year? It's said the past comes back to visit this time of year. Maybe for the month, maybe for just one night. Some believe that spirits stick around due to "unfinished business." But why? For young Emily and her family, they would quickly find out just what "unfinished business" was waiting for them in their new home in the sleepy Adirondack town of Tupper Lake.

"Alright that's the final box. I'm all moved in!" Emily shouted down the stairs to her mom and dad, who were unpacking boxes in the kitchen below.

Her family just moved north to the Adirondacks to the town of Tupper Lake for a quiet life in the mountains surrounded by nature, lakes, rivers, and endless woods. They bought a home built in 1908. Her dad, a 6'2", 210-pound man with a long brown beard, worked construction and built log homes. He had big plans to update the one-hundred-year-old home, while her mother was a homemaker. It was their dream to live a simple life, with acres of land nestled in the Adirondack Mountains. They were finally living their dream.

It was the middle of October. The fall foliage was at peak, and the colors were magnificent. Life was looking good, especially for eight-year-old Emily, who, for the first time, had a bedroom all to herself. She was free to decorate the room however she pleased. A thrill for any little girl. However, that thrill would change as the weeks went on.

The family spent the first couple days enjoying their new home and the beautiful scenery around town. Picturesque fall days outside exploring the local trails, and chilly nights sitting around the campfire in their backyard. They were living the mountain-life they moved north for. The joy of their new home, however, would take a strange turn that third night.

As Emily climbed into bed, her dad, a logger-turned-contractor, tucked her in and asked, "So what do you think of your new room?"

With childlike joy, she replied, "It's better than I imagined. And look! Mom and I even put some stars up today," pointing to the ceiling.

He looked at the glow-in-the-dark stars scattered throughout the freshly painted sheetrock and responded, "Perfect, now you can sleep under the stars every night." He kissed her goodnight, turned off the light, and walked down the upstairs hallway to his bedroom, curiously observing the ceilings in the other rooms.

"Emily's room is the only one in the house with sheetrock. How strange," he said to his wife. They hit the hay early that night, just after 9:00. They had another long day ahead of them, unpacking and turning their dream mountain house into their dream mountain home.

Meanwhile, Emily stared at her star-covered ceiling, imagining that she was somewhere in the woods camping. She eventually dozed off in her new room, a room all to herself . . . or so she thought . . .

A few hours went by. Leaves could be heard blowing around outside through her cracked window. Suddenly a loud *crash* awoke Emily from a dead sleep. She turned her head to see the silhouette of a woman in a long, torn-up dress walking across her bedroom. Frightened, she closed her eyes, pulled the covers over her head, and screamed out to her dad.

Her parents came running. The bedroom door flew open, and they flipped on the light switch to discover a set of folding attic stairs laid out from the ceiling to the floor along the wall next to Emily's bed. Broken sheetrock laid across her floor as dust particles filled the air.

"Old houses have lots of secrets," Emily's dad said. "This attic entrance must have been closed up at some point," he continued. He told Emily that the fresh paint must have weakened the sheetrock, causing it to fall.

"We will clean this up in the morning," Emily's mom said with a yawn before giving her another kiss goodnight.

Due to the commotion of the staircase, Emily didn't tell her parents about the woman's silhouette she saw. After another hour, Emily's nerves were still high. Her eyes moved back and forth across her room, looking for the woman's silhouette, but she eventually fell back to sleep.

The next morning her father cleaned up the mess. Emily told her mother about the woman she saw walking around her bedroom. "That woman was a figment of your imagination," her mom explained. "It was just a shadow caused by the falling stairs. There's nothing to be scared of."

After Emily's father finished cleaning up the sheetrock and reattaching the mystery staircase above her ceiling, Emily went about her day as kids tend to do. She explored her new home both inside and out. As bedtime approached, however, Emily was cautious going to sleep. Her mother assured her once again there was nothing to be afraid of, so off to sleep she went.

Like clockwork, at the exact same time as the previous night, Emily awoke to the sound of the attic stairs opening once again. There wasn't a crash this time around, however, just a slow creak as the stairs were pulled down to the floor. Emily sat up with a jolt just in time to see the decapitated heads of a woman and a young girl roll across the foot of her bed as the silhouette of a mother and daughter walked up the attic stairs. A fountain of fluorescent red blood came flowing out from under her bed like a river stream. She screamed at the top of her lungs.

Her mother came running into the room, flipped on the lights, and saw the blood on the floor flowing around her daughter's bed. Quickly she scooped Emily up and ran out of the room, passing Emily's father as he made his way in. Half-asleep, he stepped into the room to see what all the fuss was over. Moments later, as he opened the bedroom door, he saw the blood-stained floor with his own eyes.

Terrified and in shock, Emily waited in her parents' room with her mother. Her father ran back and told his wife to come back to Emily's bedroom. Nervously she followed him down the hallway to Emily's bedroom, where they entered to see . . . nothing. The blood was gone, the heads were nowhere to be found, and the staircase was mysteriously folded back into the ceiling as though nothing had happened. The 2" × 4" brace her father installed that morning under the folded stairs was back in place.

Emily and her family quickly packed their car and left the house to stay with a nearby friend. As they drove, Emily quietly told her parents, "I saw the woman in the ripped dress last night." Her parents exchanged a look of dread. Silence filled the air.

The next morning, Emily's father left for work. Emily and her mother went to the local library searching for information and answers about their new house. They looked up old newspapers with their address and learned that the home was built by a lumberjack as a gift to his wife in the early 1900s. His wife lived there happily for years, raising their four-year-old daughter, while the lumberjack split his time between home and lumbering camps throughout the Adirondacks. Unexpectedly one lumber season, the husband did not return home with his group. No one had any answers—he simply vanished. Many assumed he probably lost his footing, fell in the river, and drowned under the log flow, a sad reality of the times and profession. Others claimed to have seen him deep in conversation with a group of travelers not long before he disappeared.

Heartbroken, the lumberjack's widow spent the next year desperately searching for clues that might lead to her missing spouse. Then, on an unseasonably cold mid-October morning, someone entered their house in the middle of the night and beheaded both the woman and their daughter with an axe. The bloodied murder weapon was left at the scene, with the name of the missing lumberjack carved into its splintered wooden handle.

A week went by before Emily and her parents nervously returned to their home. Emily refused to sleep in her new bedroom, and ironically was back sleeping in her parents' bedroom. She felt safe with them.

Life went on for the young family, although that fateful mid-October night remained in their minds, altering the perfect Adirondack mountain life they expected. The presence in the 1900s log home never quite felt right. Their dream house no longer felt like their dream home.

A couple months passed, as the early-December snow settled in, when Emily and her family received a mysterious package in the mail. It was an old handwritten diary from the 1930s that belonged to a thirteen-year-old girl who used to live in that house. Her bedroom was Emily's bedroom. The entries contained similar accounts to Emily's tale of a headless woman and young girl coming and going from the attic. This left the family stunned as they wondered who sent this package.

Furthermore, it confirmed that her family had attempted to seal and conceal the attic back in the 1930s in the hopes of ridding the home of the spirits who lived there. It didn't work. The thirteen-year-old's family eventually had enough and sold the house, leaving behind the nightmare once and for all.

That January, just a few months after moving in, Emily's family left the home and moved to Long Lake. Sadly, their Tupper Lake house sat untouched and unsold for years until it mysteriously burned to the ground.

To this day, no one knows if it was the lumberjack or a stranger who murdered the young family. Did something sinister happen to the lumberjack during the long winter at camp, and then to cover their tracks, the murderer went after his kin and left the axe to frame him? Was his wife getting too close to discovering a truth someone didn't want discovered? It's hard to say. Whatever the case, reports still come in from time to time of people seeing the headless ghosts of a woman and a young daughter wandering the railroad tracks near the old footprint of their home in Tupper Lake.

It's often said that spirits stay in this world due to unfinished business. Could the ghost of the lumberjack's wife be searching for her long-lost husband? Maybe. Was it the lumberjack who brutally murdered his own widow and daughter with an axe? Or was it someone else? We may never know. But we can be sure these two lost souls will be searching for answers this October as they desperately seek the lumberjack—a girl's father, a widow's husband—in both this world and the next.

CHAPTER EIGHT

THE FIVE PONDS BIGFOOT

A TRUE STORY

This true story took place in the mid-1980s in the Five Ponds Wilderness, located in the western Adirondacks. The story has been told to me and written directly for this book.

It was late October, when my friend and I were at my hunting camp for a couple days of deer hunting in the Five Ponds Wilderness, in the Star Lake/Cranberry Lake region. The camp is many miles back in the woods, accessible only by four-wheelers.

We wasted no time upon arriving at the camp and got an early-morning hunt in. We even landed a buck on our first day at camp. After field-dressing the deer, we brought it back to the camp and began the process of hanging it up overnight, which is typical practice for harvesting a deer. Because I've hunted out of this camp for years, we had a system in place for hanging deer just outside the front door of the cabin. There were two large pine trees connected by a twelve-foot steel pipe wedged and tied on top of branches roughly fifteen feet up, forming an *H* shape. This allowed us to hang a deer in the middle of the pipe, far enough away from each tree so that a climbing bear couldn't touch it and high enough off the ground to keep anything else from getting to it.

We brought the deer back to camp and hung it up on the pipe, which held many deer over the years. It was business as usual, you could say, as the deer hung five feet over our heads. It was still the middle of the afternoon when we finished, so we decided to head into town and come back in the morning to process the deer. Because it was October, the temperatures were low enough the meat wouldn't spoil overnight. We hopped on our four-wheelers and drove a few miles out of the woods back to town.

The next morning, we came back to the camp with more supplies. Upon arriving, something felt off. We immediately discovered the hanging deer was gone. It vanished without a trace, but even more peculiar, the entire pipe and pulley system was gone, too. Having hunted at this camp for years, I never experienced anything like this. There's never anybody out here, especially this deep in these woods. This didn't make any sense to me. The ladder we store behind the cabin to hang the deer was completely untouched.

We surveyed the entire area around the camp and throughout the thick woods, but we didn't find any signs of footprints in the dirt or mud, just our own. Left scratching our heads and frustrated from the stolen deer, there was nothing more we could do about it at this point. Our deer was gone, so we went back into the woods and did some more hunting later that day. Unfortunately, we didn't experience the same luck on day 2 that we did twenty-four hours earlier. So after a long day sitting in a tree stand, we went back to the cabin empty-handed. This time of year, the sun usually set around 6:00 p.m. We made dinner and went to sleep around 9:00. This was the beginning of what would become the most terrifying night of my life.

A few hours later, as we slept soundly inside the modest cabin, a giant slap hit the outside wall, so loud it immediately awoke both of us from a dead sleep. "Did you hear that?" I whispered to my buddy, who nodded his head yes.

We both stayed silent in our bunks and listened to the dead night air. Our eyes searched around the cabin and out the windows into the dark woods. Moments later, as we sat in silence, we heard heavy footsteps walking around the outside of the cabin. *Thud, thud, thud.* Whatever was out there was big and heavy. Suddenly, another loud, powerful slap hit the exterior cabin wall right behind where I was laying. We both jumped out of our beds and ran to the center of the room. Someone or something was outside the cabin.

At this point, chaos ensued. The walls of the cabin began to violently shake, and the building started to sway, almost as if it was being lifted off the ground. Everything inside the kitchen cabinets came spilling out onto the old wooden floor, crashing down and shattering. The slapping on the walls continued. It was mayhem. The attack lasted for a few minutes but felt like an eternity. What was a quiet, peaceful evening just minutes earlier now turned into violent chaos that had us frightened for our lives. Scared, confused, and panicked I grabbed my .444 rifle and told my buddy to open the front door. "I'm going to fire some shots outside!" I yelled.

Filled with anxiety, he opened the front door, and I immediately shot off a few rounds into the dark night sky to scare off whomever (or whatever) was wreaking havoc on the camp. At this point, my friend let go of the front door, and because of the chaos and being as scared as I was, I kept firing off rounds as the wooden door closed. I even shot two bullets right through the front door of the cabin.

The night became silent once again. The madness outside the cabin had come to an end as suddenly as it had started. Whatever was slapping the building and shaking the walls like an earthquake was gone. We both stayed inside and stood in the center of the cabin for more than an hour, clenching our rifles, frightened that whatever was outside would come back for round 2. It never did. However, we were both too scared to stay inside and felt we would be safer higher up, on the cabin roof.

It took a little while of working up our courage, but eventually, we ran outside, grabbed the ladder from behind the cabin, and climbed up onto the roof. We stayed up there for the entire night. I'm not sure why, but we felt safer up there and would have a fighting chance if this creature returned rather than sitting inside the cabin. We waited out the night sitting on the shingles, rifles in hand. We eventually dozed off to sleep up on the slope of the roof. The sun rose with no other incidents. We left camp first thing in the morning.

My family still uses this hunting camp, and the two bullet holes in the front door can be seen to this day. I have only told this story a couple times. It makes me extremely uncomfortable to relive that fateful night in the Five Ponds Wilderness because it brings back awful memories. I feel like the story needs to be told and people need to know what's in the woods. I have experienced other bizarre things in this area of the ADK, such as whoops and tree knocks on numerous occasions. Another time, I heard something large walking through the water on two legs around midnight, and then shortly after that, I saw two different sets of glowing red eyes in the woods that were at least eight feet high.

The woods are a very different place at night, and there's something different out there in the Five Ponds Wilderness.

CHAPTER NINE

THE NYE WOLF RETURNS

Winter. A lonely time of year when the world comes to a screeching halt and time stands still. The days are short, and the nights are long. The frozen lakes and snow-covered mountains fill the landscape. A time of year when one misstep could be the difference between a fun backcountry adventure or an untimely death. Winter is the season of death, after all. It's also the time of year when the creatures of the woods expand their territory as they travel farther and farther in the name of survival.

Now, these mountains are no place for the weak or the unprepared. Year after year, backcountry travelers get swallowed alive by this unforgiving, dismal wilderness. Some hikers, skiers, and climbers go missing, never to be seen again. It's a rugged land that is not to be tested. Those who disrespect its power always lose. But there's more out there than just the harsh, unforgiving conditions. Something else roams these mysterious mountains, seeking to swallow up the unprepared. Sometimes it's even a race to see what strikes first: the mountains . . . or the wolf. For Paul and his brother Alex, a miscalculated winter day on the MacIntyre Range will prove to be a day they'll never forget—that is, if they can make it out of the woods alive.

It was a mid-December afternoon as winter began to take shape all around the Northeast. Snow was falling in the Adirondack Mountains, and that meant it was time for a winter adventure. The college semester was complete, and Christmas vacation was in full effect. "What better way to start the long break from classes and responsibilities than a spontaneous outdoors adventure," Paul thought to himself as he loaded up his beat-up, trusty gold Toyota Corolla. Paul's younger brother Alex threw his backpack into the car before he reluctantly closed the trunk.

"Are you sure we have everything we need?" Alex asked, hopping into the passenger seat. "Aren't these mountains covered in snow?"

"Look around!" Paul confidently replied. "The ground is bare, and it's fifty degrees out. Winter has barely begun. We'll be fine."

Paul started the car, and the journey north from Westchester County had officially begun. They planned to drive that day to the Adirondack Loj parking lot, where they'd spend the night in their car at the trailhead to enjoy an early start. They heard from several friends how great the MacIntyre Range was, and after seeing summit photos over the summer, they needed to experience it themselves. So off they went. Their end-of-semester ADK adventure had begun.

They only made it one hundred miles up I-87 before the sleep-deprived college-student life took effect. The boys decided to sleep at a rest stop instead and finish the drive to the trailhead in the morning. They were fast asleep with the front seats reclined, the car heat blasting, hats on, and wearing their jackets like blankets. The morning sun soon arrived, but instead of waking up in the woods to the sound of birds and hikers preparing for adventure, they awoke to the sound of semitrucks along the highway.

"Not quite the morning vibe I was promised," Alex said to his older brother as they stumbled out of the car to stretch their legs in the chilly morning air.

They ate some food they brought, hopped back into the gold Corolla, and continued north. They were still hours from the trailhead, so the day was already behind schedule. This didn't concern the two brothers, though, and before they knew it, they were passing the beloved "Now entering Adirondack Park" sign.

"Almost there!" Paul excitedly said to his brother.

The boys soon found themselves seeing more and more snow the farther north they drove, which caused some alarm for Alex. "You said there was barely any snow up here!" Alex said. "There's so much snow!"

Paul was just as surprised but unfazed. "Oh, it's fine. It's just snow," he replied confidently. "We have boots and coats, right?"

Despite Paul's confidence, Alex was not convinced "Are you sure that's all we need?" he asked. "Those people on Everest always have snowshoes and bright-colored jackets and goggles on."

Paul replied, "Yeah, oh well. We'll just wing it."

A few hours after waking, the boys pulled into the Adirondack Loj parking lot. What was supposed to be an 8:00 a.m. start time turned into an 11:00 a.m. start, but the brothers quickly suited up. As they were writing their names in the trailhead registry, a forest ranger on cross-country skis came up the trail and called out, "Hey, guys, late start, huh?"

"Yeah, we're about three hours behind, but hey, better late than never, right?" he said with a cheeky smile.

Unamused, the ranger advised the boys that it may be a good day to alter their plans, with the impending weather arriving that night mixed with their late start and lack of equipment.

"Thanks for the tip, but we'll be fine," Paul replied as he turned and started walking up the trail.

Paul and Alex were both dressed in denim jeans, winter boots, hooded sweatshirts, backpacks, and winter jackets. They both had a couple liters of water and some granola bars for snacks.

"Are you sure we have what we need to climb mountains?" Alex said as they began walking along the trail. "I mean we don't even have snowshoes."

"We have what we have: coats, some food and water, boots," Paul responded. "We have GPS on our phones, and we don't need snowshoes. Look around. There's only an inch of snow on the ground."

Alex followed his older brother's lead, and they continued hiking along the trail.

The season was unusually warm until this point, with minimal snow around the Adirondacks. The ground and trees were still covered with fluffy, white snow, creating the picturesque winter wonderland they anticipated. They made it to the Algonquin Trail split a mile from the trailhead and turned right to head up the MacIntyre Range.

"These GPS apps are impressive," Paul said. "This will be easy."

Their plan for the day was to climb to Algonquin, Iroquois, and Wright, known as the MacIntyre Range. As the two continued getting higher in elevation, they found themselves constantly slipping and sliding along the abundance of small boulders and rocks that line the Algonquin Trail. They found themselves struggling more than anticipated on the icy rocks, and the snow was getting deeper the higher they climbed.

"OK, let's stop and take a break. I need some food," Alex said to his older brother, who was brushing the snow off his half-frozen jeans.

Upon stopping, the boys saw something big and dark move across the trail up ahead. "Whoa, did you see that!" Paul exclaimed. "I think that was a bear. It was black."

This put Alex on edge, but he quickly wrote it off as a joke. "Very funny. You wish it was a bear," Alex replied, taking his water bottle out of his pack. When he grabbed the bottle, though, Alex learned that his water was frozen solid. Paul's water was not quite frozen over yet, so they shared a small sip of water and some granola bars.

"OK, now I'm freezing," Alex said. "We need to keep moving."

Paul was cold, too, but didn't want to admit it. The temperatures kept dropping as their elevation increased. They continued up the Algonquin Trail, having already sweat through their sweatshirts, slipping and falling every few steps. Their jeans froze more. The late start was catching up to the boys, and because the days were shorter this time of year, they didn't have nearly the same amount of daylight to enjoy.

Two hours into the hike, they arrived at the Wright Peak trail junction marked by a brown wooden sign with yellow letters. Exhausted and dehydrated, the boys took another break. The trail sign at the junction read, "Wright Peak 0.4 miles, Algonquin 0.7 miles." The boys headed up Wright Peak first.

As the two began climbing, Alex felt uneasy, as if something was following them. He heard footsteps in the snow directly behind him, but each time he turned around, expecting to see another hiker, no one was there. The only tracks in the snow were their own. To make it worse, every time he did turn around, he was met with a huge gust of snow and wind in his face.

"Paul, do you feel like something is following us?" Alex cautiously asked his brother.

"Probably just other hikers," Paul replied as he brushed off his brother's question.

Up the mountain the boys went, leaving the tree line and heading onto the exposed rock that began the final trek to the summit. The wind was howling, the snow was deep and heavy, and their visibility was limited, but they made it. It was a short-lived summit stay, however, thanks to the intense snow squalls. The boys took a few photos and immediately headed back down the trail. It was a challenge to navigate, but they followed the giant cairns and their nearly covered footprints back toward the trail inside the tree line.

On top of the weather conditions, the boys had other challenges. Without any traction on their feet, the brothers had a hellish time getting back down. Slippery ice and steep mountain slopes made for a bad combination. Halfway from the summit to the tree line, Paul slipped on a patch of ice and slid more than twenty-five feet. He desperately tried to cling to anything he could as he slid helplessly down the exposed rock face. Panicked, he did whatever he could to stop the slide, digging his feet in and grabbing the ground with both hands so hard he lost a glove in the process. He stopped when he landed against a five-foot-tall cairn.

"Are you OK?" Alex yelled from above. Paul was dazed and couldn't see or hear Alex due to the heavy wind and snow blowing around him.

The boys didn't have goggles, so their visibility was extremely limited as the exposed mountain conditions continued to pummel them. After a minute, Paul was able to compose himself and stand up as Alex finally made his way down. "Are you OK?" Alex yelled, as he approached a visibly shaken Paul. "Here, you might want this," Alex said, handing Paul the glove he lost during the slide. Paul was in such a high-adrenaline state that he didn't notice his missing glove or that his entire right palm was bloody and sliced up from trying to stop the slide.

"Well, that's not good," Alex said as he saw the blood.

"Wow, I didn't even notice. It's fine," Paul said, before the two continued their way down the open ledges and back into the tree line.

Before they knew it, the brothers were back at the Wright Peak trail junction. They stopped again to compose themselves before Alex proposed a change in their plan. "Hey, let's just skip the other two mountains today," he suggested. "We're wet and frozen, you're bleeding, and it's getting late already."

Paul contemplated his brother's proposition but was too focused on the task at hand. "We're only 0.7 miles away and we've come this far," Paul responded firmly. "I'm going to Algonquin."

Suddenly a large gust of wind whipped in as the boys covered their faces. "I think that's a sign that it's time to head back to the trailhead," Alex stated as he wiped the freshly blown snow off his face. "Plus, your hand is shredded."

Paul was dead set on summiting a second mountain and suggested that Alex head back to the car. He would *quickly* run up to summit Algonquin and leave Iroquois for another day. "I'll be an hour behind you at most," Paul ignorantly claimed. "I have my phone's map and flashlight. I'll be fine."

So after the compromise to alter their plan, the brothers split up. Alex headed down the mountain to the trailhead, and Paul kept climbing toward Algonquin. Despite the frozen jeans, sweaty clothes, and frozen water, Paul was determined to summit Algonquin. Unbeknownst to him, however, the trail was about to get a whole lot harder.

It was the middle of the afternoon when Alex continued down the trail, making his way toward the trailhead and wondering if it was a bad idea to have split up. Down the trail proved harder than climbing up because he didn't have any traction on his shoes, a lesson the brothers were both learning the hard way.

Meanwhile, Paul was ascending the mountain surrounded by the abundance of snow-covered evergreens that helped block the treacherous winds. While he was climbing, he felt the hair on the back of his neck stand up, and he couldn't shake the feeling that something was following him, just like his brother was talking about. He swore he could hear footsteps in the snow directly behind him, but when he turned around, no one was there. Just his footsteps and a giant gust of wind every time. He wrote it off as nerves and continued hiking up the trail, slipping and sliding with nearly every step. Every so often, he heard heavy footsteps running up behind him, only to vanish the moment he turned around. "This is weird," Paul thought to himself.

The afternoon temperature continued to drop, and his wet clothes continued to freeze. This 0.7 miles felt like an eternity, but he was about to break the tree line once again for the final push to the summit out on the open, exposed rock for a quarter-mile.

"OK, here we go!" Paul said to himself, stepping onto the exposed mountaintop, only to be immediately hit with snow squalls limiting his visibility dramatically. The flurries were blinding, the wind was blowing, and the snow was waist deep as Paul trudged along step by step. The only way he could find any sense of a trail to the summit was looking for the giant cairns he remembered following on the way up Wright Peak earlier. He eventually spotted one in the distance and headed toward it. Each step was met with a large amount of effort as he sank nearly to his waist. Traveling in these conditions with snowshoes is a daunting task; without them, it was nearly impossible to move.

Paul fell face first into the snow from pure exhaustion and early signs of hypothermia. To make matters worse, he couldn't see his footprints anymore thanks to the hurricane-like wind. The mighty mountain was roaring as Paul sat there, helpless in the snow, frozen, surrounded by heavy winds, completely and utterly lost with twilight setting in.

Paul didn't know what to do, he didn't know which way to go to get back to the tree line, and he didn't know where the trail was. As he contemplated his situation, he caught movement in his peripheral vision. To the west, a black figure on four legs was walking along the mountain slope. Between the wind and blowing snow, he couldn't quite make out what it was. The only thing he knew for certain was that whatever it was, it was moving right toward him.

Back down at the base of the mountain, Alex arrived at the trailhead. Exhausted, frozen, and badly in need of food and water, he, too, was in an early stage of hypothermia. Fortunately, he was able to get into the car, change his clothes, and warm his body up. Figuring Paul was only going to be an hour behind him, Alex had no problem sitting in the warm car and eating some snacks as he waited for his brother to get off the mountain. He called Paul's phone to check in, but there was no answer.

The hurricane-like winds continued to rip across the landscape, as Paul frantically searched for a sign of the trail. He was fully lost on the exposed mountain, in high winds, in frozen clothes, waist deep snow, and hypothermic. Their exciting mountain adventure had turned into a disaster on the brink of tragedy. Paul continued crawling up the mountain, desperately looking for a cairn or a sign of his footsteps to lead him back down. The black figure was visible once again, and it was gaining on him, slowly but methodically moving toward him, getting closer and closer with every gust of wind. To make matters worse, the sun began to set behind the western High Peaks. Paul knew he was in trouble, and he didn't know where to go or what to do. His body and mind were shutting down, and then he collapsed.

Meanwhile, at the trailhead, Alex's concern grew, seeing no sign of Paul two and half hours later. Something was wrong. He grabbed his cell phone and called him but no answer. It was time to report his missing brother. He dialed a number he got off the trailhead register . . .

"DEC."

"Hi, I need to report a missing hiker."

The wind started to die down as the darkness set in on Algonquin. Paul regained consciousness, partially buried in the snow, frozen, and with no idea which direction to go. He stumbled to his feet, and suddenly those familiar heavy footsteps returned behind him. This time, though, they were accompanied by a low, guttural growl. The mysterious dark figure had arrived. A large black wolf towered over Paul, its one purple eye staring straight into his. The wolf flashed its long fangs and growled viciously as it began circling Paul, methodically, planning the attack on his prey. Paul's fear turned to panic as his body was struggling to move in the deep snow.

The wolf continued to growl and flash its large teeth, circling closer and closer to Paul, while Paul's vision was going blurry. In and out of focus, the wolf staged its attack. It let out one giant growl, and Paul flinched and covered his head. But nothing happened. He opened his eyes and scanned the perimeter, but the wolf was gone. The air was quiet now.

After letting out one breath of relief, the growl was back from above, and the wolf attacked! Jumping onto Paul, the battle was underway. The wolf viciously latched onto Paul's right hand while the two rolled around in the snow. Paul was able to pry open the clenched jaws of the beast, and he tossed the wolf away down the mountainside into the darkness. Paul made a run for it up the mountain before it attacked again.

He trudged through the snow, constantly looking over his shoulder for any sign of the black wolf or that glowing purple eye. Soon Paul found a rock wall and backed up to it before turning around. He was trapped, and the wolf was nowhere to be seen. The air was soft now as a gentle breeze blew. The darkness filled the night sky. Paul was fighting more than just the wolf as hypothermia continued to set in . . .

"Yes, he thought he would be an hour behind me at most," said Alex from the inside of his car to their father on the phone. "Have you heard from him?" No sign from Paul as the night set in. Knowing he was frozen and without a real flashlight, they feared the worst.

The air was cold yet still on the summit of Algonquin. The clouds opened, and the moon and stars filled the sky. The temperature continued to drop. Paul stood against the rock, looking down the mountain for the wolf, unsure where he should go. His body was shutting down, and it was a battle to keep his brain vigilant. It was only a matter of time now for Paul, as the reality of his fate set in. He was cold. He was alone. What was going to take him first: the mountain or the wolf? His hand continued to bleed thanks to the battle with the wolf, but that was the least of his concerns now. Where did the wolf go? Was he about to die alone on this mountain? The mountain that was supposed to provide a simple adventure was looking like it would be marking the end of his life's adventure.

Moments later, Paul sat alone in the darkness, and he heard that familiar sound once again: heavy footsteps approaching him. He was without a flashlight, and the only light he had was from the moon. The footsteps grew heavier and louder, and the low growls that followed were getting bigger and angrier. The wolf was back to finish what it started.

Paul's mind was shutting down as the growls surrounded him from every direction. Paul was too weak to fight. He prepared himself for the worst. He continued looking around the mountain for that purple glow.

In his final moments, Paul caught movement in his blurry peripheral vision—a light. This light, however, wasn't purple; it was a different glow. It was yellow. The light was accompanied by multiple voices yelling, "Paul! Paul, where are you?"

His heroes had arrived! The rangers made it just in the nick of time. Suddenly, the fear of the wolf vanished as quickly as the wolf itself, and Paul muscled up the strength for one loud yell: "Help!" They heard his cries. He was saved!

Paul was in and out of consciousness as the rangers loaded him into a helicopter down the mountain. He was immediately taken out of his wet clothes and put into warm clothes, fed food and water, and driven by ambulance to the hospital for further treatment.

While being treated for hypothermia, Paul's nurse noticed his hands and asked, "What happened to your right hand? It was covered in blood?"

Paul looked down at the injured hand. "Oh, I scraped it pretty badly on the ice and rocks when I slid down the mountain," he said. "My glove fell off midslide."

The nurse continued, "I see. It looked like you were attacked by a dog or something. Those look like teeth marks on the back of your hand."

Paul turned his bandaged hand over and examined it. The memories began flooding his brain. The footsteps, the black wolf, the purple eye, the attack. As his nurse was leaving his room, Paul asked, "Nurse, are there wolves here in the Adirondacks?"

The nurse gently laughed to herself as she flipped the light off. "You've been through a lot today," she said. "Get some rest."

Deep in the High Peaks Wilderness lurks more than just the occasional black bear and coyote. Something more diabolic and cunning roams these woods. Something that stalks its prey and wears them down until they're too weak to fight back. Something that patiently waits for the unsuspecting hiker to make the wrong move. His footsteps are right behind you, but you'll never see them. He's too smart to leave a trace. He's too shrewd to let you see him before the attack. The next time you hear a noise behind you or you feel a gust of wind, you may want to be on alert. You'll know he's close by. Are you the prey he's after?

When you do hear that gust of wind, it's time to get out of the woods. The Nye Wolf preys on the unsuspecting and often unprepared hiker. He's smart like that. Sometimes, however, it's not the Nye Wolf you need to worry about the most; it's the mountains. For some unlucky hikers, there's a fight between the wolf and the Adirondack mountains for who will claim you first. Will the wolf get to them before the mountain does? For Paul and Alex, you can be sure they're not going to put themselves in such a deadly predicament again. Because next time, the mountains and the wolf may not show the same mercy they showed that fateful December day.

ADIRONDACK FOLKLORE

CHAPTER TEN

THE LADY IN THE LAKE

←——————— ≪ • ≫ ———————→

Perhaps one of the best-known Adirondack legends, "The Lady in the Lake" recounts the tragic tale of Mabel Douglass Smith, a successful professional woman who was the first dean of the New Jersey College for Women at Rutgers. The story is not cut and dry, as conflicting versions of the tale exist. It is undisputed, however, that the peaceful, serene Lake Placid, a 5.5-mile-long lake in the heart of the Adirondacks, became the sight of a mystery that has remained unsolved for almost a century.

While Mabel had received professional accolades for her accomplishments in education at the school that would later become Douglass College, her personal life was in shambles. Her husband's untimely death in 1917, followed by her son's death by suicide six years later, led to Mabel's mental breakdown. She entered a mental health facility for a year and was taken by her daughter to the family's home, Camp Onondaga, on Lake Placid for respite after her release.

On September 21, 1933, the women planned to return home to New Jersey after closing the camp for the season. Mabel told her daughter she was going to collect the fall leaves for decoration before returning home and set off onto Lake Placid in the family's rowboat. Tragically, her two-mile paddle was her last, and she was not seen again for thirty years.

On September 15, 1963, a group of scuba divers were exploring one of the deepest parts of Lake Placid near Pulpit Rock, aptly named for its appearance as a place a minister would deliver his sermon. Two divers followed Pulpit Rock down through the water's depths, first discovering an old guide boat on a rock shelf. Then, nearly one hundred feet below the water's surface, they discovered an eerie, white figure. The divers believed it to be a mannequin put there as a practical joke. To their shock and horror, they quickly realized that the figure was no mannequin but a well-preserved woman's corpse. She lay on her right side with her legs together in a crouching position, and it hardly looked as if time had touched her. The divers then noticed that the corpse had a fifty-pound anchor tied around its neck with a short rope.

The body, perfectly preserved underwater, had a white, waxy appearance, tricking the divers into initially believing she was made of plastic. It is speculated that Douglass's corpse was so well preserved upon discovery due to the freezing temperatures of her watery grave, as well as the mineral content of the water. The first diver motioned for his partner to stay with the body while he returned to the surface to mark the location of the corpse so police could later investigate. However, as the young diver waited in Lake Placid's dark depths, he became unsettled about Mabel's lifelike appearance. Unnerved and thinking she could wake up any second, the diver decided to bring the body to the surface himself, but as he attempted to bring the corpse to the surface, the woman's arms and head detached, and her facial features disintegrated.

Because Mabel's disappearance was the only unsolved one in Lake Placid, investigators were able to determine that the recovered corpse off Pulpit Rock belonged to her. However, by the time Douglass's body was recovered, she had no living relatives to claim her. Douglass's daughter, Edith, committed suicide in 1948 after the disappearance of her mother and the death of her own husband. Officials from Douglass College, then named in her honor, handled the funeral arrangements. Douglass was buried in Brooklyn's Green-Wood Cemetery, which is also the gravesite of her husband and children.

The official cause of Mabel Douglass Smith's death was accidental drowning. She was rowing an unstable boat, and it's possible that she may have slipped and fallen, unintentionally entangling herself in the anchor's rope. Conversely, many consider that the devastation in Douglass's personal life led her to take her own life on that fateful day in

September 1933. Although her body was exhumed, it is speculated that Douglass's spirit still haunts her watery tomb. Many boaters and campers on Lake Placid have reported seeing the ghostly figure of a woman hovering near Pulpit Rock. These individuals have kept the legend of the Lady in the Lake alive for nearly a century. While the true fate of Mabel Douglass Smith may forever remain a mystery, it is certain that the legend of her tragic death will remain in Adirondack lore for decades to come.

CHAPTER ELEVEN

BIGFOOT IN THE ADIRONDACKS

If there was ever a place where a tall, bipedal, scientifically undiscovered creature could exist undetected, the Adirondack Mountains would be the place. A vast, mostly unpopulated, rugged wilderness filled with unlimited food and cover. Perhaps this is why, year after year, more people report seeing something in the woods. Something they can't explain. Something they're told doesn't exist. A large, apelike creature walking upright on two feet. Something many have described as having the build of a professional bodybuilder with the height of a professional basketball player (or taller), yet it moves through the woods with the grace of a gymnast. Could it be possible that this creature, known typically as Sasquatch or bigfoot, truly does roam these woods? After all, every Native American tribe has talked about these creatures for centuries, so there must be something to it.

Thousands of reports from everyday people are documented around the world by researchers every year, and the Adirondack Park is no exception. From hikers to hunters to campers to people walking their dogs, sightings of these creatures happen consistently in the ADK. While this subject is often thought of as a Pacific Northwest phenomenon, sightings are reported in every state every year.

What are people experiencing, you ask? Well, that depends. Many report powerful, siren-like screaming deep in the woods. Others report having rocks thrown at them or their tent at night. Many expert hikers have described experiencing a sudden feeling of dread while hiking because they feel like they're being watched in the woods. Reports of unusual sounds, such as tree knocks, whoops, and something large crashing through the forest like a freight train, occur often. Dog owners often report their brave, carefree, adventurous dogs suddenly turning into whimpering little puppies, desperate to turn back and get out of the woods, almost as if something in the woods wasn't right and they didn't want to continue along the trail. For anyone who has a dog that lives for walks in the woods, these moments will make you wonder what's going on.

Are all these moments coincidence? Highly explainable? Possibly. But when the same types of reports are recorded every year from different people experiencing the same things, it's enough to make you wonder, "Maybe something *is* out there . . ."

Now you're probably wondering, "But what about the visual sightings?" Class A encounters are commonly reported in the Adirondack Park from locals and visitors to hunters and outdoor recreationists alike. In fact, both bigfoot stories in this very book were experienced by real people here in the park. Kind of makes you wonder, doesn't it?

Now for a little fun. Here are some recent reports of ADK bigfoot sightings recorded by the Bigfoot Field Researchers Organization (BFRO) and others:

1992: A group of hikers reported hearing strange vocalizations and seeing large footprints near their campsite in the Pharaoh Lake Wilderness. The footprints appeared to have been made by a bipedal creature and measured more than sixteen inches in length.

1996: A pair of canoers reported seeing a large, hairy creature along the shore of Pine Pond, crouched down fifty feet away (at the base of Mount Ampersand), before it stood up and started sniffing the air. The creature was brown and estimated to be seven feet tall. It ran away in the woods.

1997: A man reported seeing a large, hairy creature walking on two legs near his cabin in the Adirondacks. The creature was estimated to be around seven feet tall and was described as having long, shaggy hair.

2002: A hunter reported seeing a large, bipedal creature near Cedar River in the Adirondack Park. The hunter estimated the creature to be around seven to eight feet tall and described it as having broad shoulders and a muscular build.

2003: A group of hikers reported seeing a large, hairy creature walking on two legs near the Mount Marcy Trail in the High Peaks Wilderness. The creature was described as eight to nine feet tall and having long, matted hair.

2011: A hiker reported seeing a large, apelike creature walking on two legs near the Northville-Placid Trail in the Adirondack Park. The hiker estimated the creature to be around seven feet tall and described it as having long arms and a bulky build.

2013: A couple was camping in the Pharaoh Lake Wilderness when they heard strange vocalizations outside their tent. The next morning, they discovered large footprints that appeared to have been made by a bipedal creature.

2014: A driver hit a hairy, bipedal, apelike creature with her car around 12:30 a.m. in Hamilton County along the Sacandaga River. The creature was carrying a deer under its arm. The car was totaled in the crash, and the creature was described as dark brown and more than seven feet tall.

2015: A group of hunters reported seeing a large, hairy creature walking on two legs near West Canada Creek in the Adirondack Park. The creature was estimated to be around seven to eight feet tall and was described as having long arms and a muscular build.

2020: A camper reported seeing a creature cross the railroad tracks in front of him while camping on Long Lake. The creature was estimated to be around seven feet tall and was on two feet and covered in auburn hair.

Bigfoot encounters have been reported throughout the Adirondack Park for decades, many taking place in remote and less-populated areas within the park. Some of the hot spots inside the Blue Line include the High Peaks Wilderness, the Pharaoh Lake Wilderness, the Five Ponds Wilderness, and the West Canada Lakes Wilderness.

From hikers on the Northville-Placid Trail, to hunters in the Five Ponds and High Peaks Wilderness areas, to campers on Long Lake, to anglers in Paul Smiths, reports of large, apelike creatures happen every year. Many stay quiet about what they've seen out of caution of ridicule. Some lifelong hunters swear they'll never go back in the woods, as they find themselves traumatized by what they encountered out there.

Whatever is going on deep in the forests of the Adirondacks, moving between the trees, the mystery and phenomena surrounding Sasquatch remains. The lore of this creature will continue to keep us in wonder (and on our toes) whenever we step into the woods. Hey, for all you know, you may have even walked past a bigfoot camouflaged in the woods, watching you along the trail, and you never even knew it.

Oh, and one last thing, no person on earth has ever actually mistaken a bipedal, apelike creature for a bear. So let's put that narrative to bed.

CHAPTER TWELVE

ADIRONDACK ELIXIR

The Adirondacks, where the fresh mountain air is crisp, clean, and refreshing, where the clear, endlessly flowing water can actually cure what ails you. Wait a minute—water that can heal the human body, in the Adirondacks? That's what William D. Hough, founder of the Chases Community, near what is now Lowville, New York, a small town at the foothills of the western Adirondacks, claimed in the early twentieth century. The source: Hinching's Pond, a small kettle lake located a mile and a half southeast of Chases.

William D. Hough (1879–1979) was a wise and talented man with many business ventures. His early endeavors were in the sand, stone, and gravel business, and he later owned an electrical contracting business. In 1922, at the age of forty-three, Hough purchased a 1,500-acre area of land that contained Chases Lake, Hinching's Pond, and Parson's Pond. With Chases Lake at the center of his land holding, he began to survey and develop the surrounding acreage. In 1933, property sales began of the holdings, which he had named Lingerlong Estates.

In keeping with his entrepreneurial spirit, Hough began promoting what he believed to be the healing properties of the water from Hinching's Pond. The pond itself is only fifty feet deep and eighteen acres in area, and it is naturally acidic. It is wholly spring fed and has no recognizable inlet or outlet. The bright blue, extraordinarily clear waters, however, contain very little wildlife. Adirondack folklore holds that Mohawk

Native Americans, who traveled between the Mohawk and St. Lawrence Rivers, made detours to this very pond for its curative properties on their voyages.

During the 1930s, thousands of gallons of Hinching's Pond water were sold for its medicinal properties. Hough and others touted the water's curative assets, and written endorsements from satisfied patients testified to the water's healing abilities. It is said that the water effectively treated skin diseases, ulcers, cataracts, lumbago, dropsy, piles, cancers, and arthritis upon ingestion. One physician, Dr. William Wright, who practiced at Marcy State Hospital in Marcy, New York, is said to have ordered hundreds of gallons of the pond's elixir throughout the 1930s to treat his patients. The doctor's notes, along with other testimonials of satisfied customers, all declare the healing powers of the Hinching's Pond water. While Hough did not allow anyone to swim in Hinching's Pond, he did ask that visitors of the pond to detail in a notebook he provided any relief that they had from drinking the pond water.

Hough lived to be just over one hundred years old and is remembered as a colorful entrepreneur in the area. Is there something to be said of the healing powers of the Hinching's Pond water, or was it simply a moneymaking scheme? Can it really cure what ails you? Mr. William D. Hough believed so, along with many others, but you'll just have to take his word for it. That, or make the trek to Hinching's Pond and try the water for yourself.

CHAPTER THIRTEEN

THE LEGEND OF CHAMP

THE LAKE CHAMPLAIN SEA MONSTER

While the Adirondack Park is most popular thanks to its mountain culture, it's equally known for its abundance of water. With thousands of bodies of water ranging from rivers to lakes to backcountry ponds, the stories lend themselves to include a little fun. With that said, it seems appropriate to talk about the sea monster of Lake Champlain.

Lake Champlain, a freshwater glacial lake, sits on the eastern edge of the Adirondacks, separating New York and the Green Mountains of Vermont. The lake is full of rich history, discovered in 1609 by French explorer Samuel D. Champlain, from whom the lake received its name. During the American Revolution, the lake was an important waterway between the New England colonies and Canada. It again played a pivotal role in the War of 1812, serving as a shipbuilding station out of Vergennes, Vermont. By 1945, the lake was bustling with tourists and today is still a source of recreation, beauty, and commerce to its surrounding regions. Crossing the lake is easy today, with several bridges spanning from New York to Vermont and three ferries crossing the lake at its wider points.

There's more to Lake Champlain's long and vibrant history, however. A story so old that some historians claim it dates to the time of Champlain's discovery more than four centuries ago. That story is of the Lake Champlain sea monster, who is reported to have been seen by Champlain in 1609. It's said that both the Iroquois and Abenaki tribes who lived along the lake also reported sightings of a mysterious sea creature. The Abenakis cautioned the French explorers against troubling the lake's waters and disturbing what they believed to be a large, horned serpent, whom they called Tatoskok. Today, the sea monster is affectionately referred to as Champ.

The creature is described as ranging in size from fifteen to fifty feet and having a long neck, a thick body, four fins, and a long tail. Many observers state that Champ resembles a plesiosaur, a marine reptile that went extinct ages ago, and still others compare Champ to the Loch Ness monster. This comparison between Champ and the Loch Ness monster, however, is more than pure coincidence. Lake Champlain and Loch Ness in Scotland share many characteristics—perhaps the ideal aquatic environment for supporting the life of an ancient sea creature. Both lakes are similar in water temperature and depth; they are long, deep, narrow, and cold. Scientists have also discovered an underwater wave called a seiche in both bodies of water that can throw underwater debris up to the lakes' surfaces. While some skeptics believe this debris is actually responsible for the sea-monster sightings, others just chalk it up to another similarity between the two lakes.

In 1977, a photograph, one that can be found in tourist shops and on postcards, was taken by Sandra Mansi that supposedly shows Champ's head and neck above the water's surface. The photograph is one of the most well-known pieces of evidence in support of Champ's existence. However, some skeptics have argued that the photograph shows nothing more than a floating log or a wave, but as with all folklore, that's for you to decide.

In 1984, a group of researchers using underwater cameras captured a video of what they claimed was Champ swimming near the shore of the lake. The video shows a long, dark shape moving through the water, but some have argued that it could be a floating log or a fish. But hey, you have to appreciate the effort though, right?

With hundreds of documented sightings on the books, Champ is synonymous with Adirondack folklore. There are many fascinating tales associated with Champ, and the lore will live on. Some locals believe that Champ is a spiritual guardian of the lake, while others think it is a prehistoric creature that somehow survived extinction. Today Champ is a beloved sea creature who even has a minor league baseball team named after him, and it continues to capture the imaginations of people far beyond the Blue Line.

Personally, I sure hope Champ is swimming around the darkest depths of Lake Champlain. It gives the lake a magical and mysterious quality that leaves me looking out my windows in wonder every time I cross it.

CHAPTER FOURTEEN

THE LEGEND OF GEORGIE

THE LAKE GEORGE SEA MONSTER

The Loch Ness monster of Scotland and Champ of Lake Champlain, New York, have become synonymous as the world's elusive sea monsters. In the summer of 1904, a lesser-known Adirondack sea monster emerged in Lake George, a thirty-two-mile-long lake located in the southern Adirondacks. The town itself, which sits on the lake of the same name, along with the neighboring villages, have been a popular summer destination and vacation spot for more than a century. The summer of 1904, though, will live on in history as one in which the entire community was nearly depopulated in light of the Lake George sea monster, appropriately named Georgie.

The sea monster's first reported sighting was at Hague Bay and later at a restaurant in nearby Hague, New York. As word spread throughout the town about the sea monster's appearance, it began to move around the lake, gaining more publicity. Where had this sea creature emerged from, and why was it choosing this summer to reveal itself from the lake's watery depths?

In the summer of 1904, two friends, artist Harry Watrous and Colonel William Mann, made a fishing bet to see who could catch the largest trout. One day, Colonel Mann passed by Watrous's house on his boat, holding up what appeared to be a fish weighing at least thirty to forty pounds. The whopper, however, turned out to be nothing more than a handcrafted fake that Mann had purchased to win the fishing wager. Not wanting Mann to get the last laugh, Watrous devised his own scheme to get back at him.

While Colonel Mann was on business in New York City in late June 1904, Watrous began work on his plot to outtrick his friend. Using a ten-foot cedar log, he attached ears that resembled a donkey's and a large mouth with two upper and two lower teeth. The eyes were made of green glass. He then painted the head yellow with black stripes, the inside of the mouth red, the teeth white, and the ears blue. Last, he painted two red spots for nostrils on what would be the nose. To the bottom of the log, Watrous rigged a hundred-foot rope with a pulley system. Using a stone as an anchor, the pulley line could be controlled from the shoreline.

Watrous then anchored the cedar log contraption along the route Colonel Mann would travel in his boat to Watrous's home along his island in Lake George. After testing the apparatus several times to ensure it was working properly, he sunk his creation and patiently waited for Mann and his friends to sail by that Saturday afternoon. To his delight, Colonel Mann had several guests onboard his boat, and upon seeing the party approach his contraption, Mann, who was hiding behind a clump of bushes on the shoreline of his property, gave the pulley rope a tug and released his monster! The head rose out of the water, shaking back and forth, an alarming sight for all onboard Colonel Mann's boat. Some of the onboard guests screamed; others repeatedly exclaimed their wonderment at the strange sight. No sooner had the boaters gotten a good look at the creature, Watrous pulled the log back underwater.

News of the mysterious sea serpent spread along the lakeshore community that evening. Under the cover of darkness, Watrous moved his cedar log creature from one place to another along the shores of Lake George. It is said that one honeymooning couple, out for a moonlit paddle, encountered Georgie, causing their canoe to capsize. The terrified groom swam to shore, leaving his new bride to ward off the sea monster herself. The seething bride eventually made her way back to the shore and is said to have stormed into the hotel, announcing the end of the honeymoon and the marriage. She was purportedly grateful to the sea monster for revealing her husband's true monstrous nature so early in the marriage.

As the creature revealed itself to more onlookers, news spread about the startling sea monster living in Lake George. Throughout the summer of 1904, Watrous was able to trick the public, and news of the sea serpent spread across New York State. And thus, Georgie was born, the illustrious sea serpent of Lake George.

The original sea monster can be seen on display at the Clifton F. West Historical Museum in the Hague Town Hall in Hague, New York. A replica of Georgie is located at the Lake George Historical Museum in Lake George, New York. While Georgie may be only a fabricated hoax, a playful gimmick between two competitive friends, the legend of the Lake George sea monster will live on in Adirondack humor and lore for summers to come.

CHAPTER FIFTEEN

THE MIRROR LAKE
ANACONDA OF 1997

←——————≪ • ≫——————→

The anaconda, an aquatic snake that inhabits tropical regions of South America, is the world's largest snake by weight and is second in length only to the reticulated python. They can grow to lengths of 30 feet, with diameters of 12 inches, and weigh up to 550 pounds. In the summer of 1997, however, this South American monster was rumored to inhabit none other than Mirror Lake, a small lake located in the heart of Lake Placid, New York.

Mirror Lake sits in the middle of the small town of Lake Placid, with the town quite literally built up around it. Main Street runs along Mirror Lake, a popular brick sidewalk spans the lake's 2.7-mile circumference, and the public beach is located along the top end of the lake's shore. The public beach was flanked on either side by two large wooden docks, separated down the middle with a deep end and shallow end, and two floating docks sat at the outer edge of the deep end.

Rumors of the Mirror Lake anaconda spread quickly through the public beachgoers, particularly among the younger crowd. There was a generalized fear, a terrible sense of dread, as the children took to the water that summer. Every splash, every accidental touch from a friend's hand or foot underwater sparked immediate terror that the anaconda was upon them, and while no one ever saw the beast, every child was sure they'd felt it brush past them as they tried to enjoy a summer afternoon at the lake.

Children across the town had heard the talk of the enormous snake that had somehow entered the water. Had someone released their pet into the lake? Had the snake escaped from some nearby terrarium, or had it slithered into one of the storm drains that emptied into the lake off Mirror Lake Drive? No one quite knew when or how the giant anaconda had made its way into the small Adirondack lake, but every child at the beach that summer was terrified it would become the snake's next meal, swallowed whole and dragged below into the watery depths, never to be seen again.

Rumors of the giant anaconda eventually fizzled out, and no one was ever eaten alive, nor was the creature ever seen. Coincidentally, the blockbuster film *Anaconda* was released in April of the same year. While the anaconda of Mirror Lake was a summer rumor, at best, the hilarity of the notion and the speed at which the rumor spread among the town's youth will live on as one of the most outlandish tales to ever come out of Lake Placid. I remember that middle school summer very well. We all swam a little faster out to the docks that year.

HOW TO TELL YOUR OWN CAMPFIRE STORY

Telling spooky stories around the campfire, whether in the backcountry or in your backyard, is a tradition that will never fade. Gathering around the fire, roasting marshmallows, and telling spooky stories about the woods is fun with the soundtrack of the crackling campfire filling the crisp night air. It's a pastime that creates memories, and memories are what live forever.

Creating your own campfire stories promotes creativity, laughter, gasps, joy, and maybe even some sleepless nights in a sleeping bag inside your tent. I want to continue this wonderful tradition and encourage you to create your own spooky tales the next time you gather 'round the fire. Here are the five basic steps I use when creating my own tall tales, and you can implement them during your next family campfire. You can even create the stories together and then have one person narrate it.

THE FIVE STEPS TO CREATING YOUR OWN CAMPFIRE STORY

1. **Pick a familiar location for the story to take place.** Choose a place that everybody around the fire knows well.
2. **Choose the antagonist. Creature, ghost, animal, person, etc.** Decide what the thing is that lives in the woods.

3. **Determine what triggers this thing to attack.** Ideas include a full moon, campers who leave their trash, unprepared hikers, swimming in a specific lake, and so on. Decide what the thing looks and sounds like. Have fun with this!

4. **Create the storyline, and bring your protagonist to the creature.** This is where you have some fun building suspense. Tell the tale in a way that allows the listener to picture themselves as the lead in the story. Campfire stories are spooky when we can envision every step of the story and picture ourselves walking the trail, swimming at the lake, smelling the pine trees, and ultimately running into the creature in the woods.

5. **Leave the story unresolved at the end.** The creature or thing must remain in the woods at the end. This will create dissonance and conflict for the listener, leaving us all wondering, "Something is *still* out there . . ."

In the end, stories that encompass a little bit of fact and a little bit of fiction are always the best ones. This allows our imaginations to paint a picture while also leaving us wondering, "Could this be true? Is this thing *really* out there?"

I hope you enjoy creating your own stories around the fire. Have fun telling them and retelling them, and let your imaginations run wild. Folklore is fun and should remain that way. Make those memories! Oh, and one last thing: Don't forget to use your best spooky campfire story voice when telling the tale!

Thank you for reading my Adirondack campfire stories. I hope to hear yours one day around the fire!

ABOUT THE AUTHOR

James Appleton is a licensed outdoors guide and Adirondack 46er who grew up in the heart of the Adirondack Mountains. He is the founder of the Lake Placid 9er hiking challenge and the host of *The 46 of 46 Podcast*, the premier outdoors podcast that brings the mountains, trails, lakes, and stories of the Adirondack Park to life.

Many listeners have referred to James as the "voice of the Adirondacks," and his demeanor, knowledge, presence, and passion for the Adirondacks continue to grow his listenership year after year. Many reviews have praised him as a "natural-born storyteller."

James and his wife, Kinnon, also an Adirondack native, live in Lake Placid, New York, with their three daughters. They love exploring the great outdoors right in their own backyard.